FILM CREW

FUNDAMENTALS of PROFESSIONAL FILM and VIDEO PRODUCTION

WRITTEN BY

NICHOLAS GEORGE

ILLUSTRATIONS BY

JESSIE L. KUNTZ

FILM CREW
Fundamentals of Professional Film and Video Production

PLATINUM EAGLE PUBLISHING
9360 W. Flamingo Road #110-133
Las Vegas, NV 89147
info@platinumeaglepublishing.com
http://platinumeaglepublishing.com

Printed in the United States of America

Library of Congress Cataloging-in-Publication Data

George, Nicholas
    Film Crew: Fundamentals of Professional Film and
Video Production / by Nicholas George — 1st Revised Edition.

ISBN 978-0-578-03344-0

Volume discounts available on books used for educational purposes. Please submit inquiries to: info@platinumeaglepublishing.com

ACKNOWLEDGEMENTS

I would like to extend my most heartfelt gratitude to all of the individuals who in any way contributed to this book, as well as those who inspired and supported me in my love of film, entertainment, and the arts along the way.

DE VEAU DUNN

JESSIE L. KUNTZ

DAVE LARSON

KATHY MCCURDY

CATHY ANDERSON

JOHN HILDEBRAND

NATE BYNUM

WILLIAM SNEAD

FRANCISCO MENENDEZ

JOHN E. HUMISTON, M.D.

LISSA MARIE MCGIVERN

EILEEN KAWA

& especially,

MOM and DAD

THANK YOU!

TABLE OF CONTENTS

Introduction

• • •

Throughout this book, the terms *Film* and *Video* are used interchangeably and should be considered synonymous as they pertain to the art form and business of capturing moving images, whether for the purpose of telling stories, conveying a message or selling a product.

It does not matter if you are participating in a film class curriculum within the context of a formal education setting, or pursuing the craft from a self-taught approach. If we are going to call ourselves filmmakers, the fact is that we are all perpetual students of the art form. Film and video production is an incredibly dynamic and fast changing medium. To succeed as a filmmaker, it is important to have as much passion for learning as for the art form itself.

Along with the technological revolution came the advent of inexpensive video cameras as well as user-friendly computer-based editing software. Thus allowing virtually anyone with a few hundred dollars and a personal computer to go out and make a movie. The general public now has access to a form of creative expression that until relatively recently was reserved for the Hollywood elite. With the barriers now gone, the art of filmmaking has become vulnerable to a "cheapening" effect. If left unchecked, this could potentially lower the expectations of the viewer in a way that compromises the overall quality of the motion picture experience that has become an indelible part of our culture.

Regardless of what great advancements in technology may bring, I strongly believe that the craft of filmmaking must continue to remain firmly rooted in the art of *storytelling*. In addition to exploring an introduction to the basic aspects of film and video production, one of the primary goals of this book is to encourage and inspire the artist within every potential filmmaker to always hold the story in the highest regard, and let it be the driving force behind all of the technical prowess that may be cultivated throughout a career in moving pictures.

Prologue

• • •

For as long as I can remember, I have had a love for storytelling and a passion for movies. My fascination with the cinema eventually led me in the direction of pursuing higher education and career endeavors that would ultimately revolve around the entertainment industry.

I first began taking classes in the areas of communications and film studies while attending college in San Diego, California. It was then that I teamed up with an already dear friend and gifted director, De Veau Dunn, to form a producer-director duo that would be the core of our San Diego based independent film crew. De Veau and I went on to work on more than a dozen independently produced film and video projects in the years that followed. I later transferred out of state to finish my studies at The University of Nevada Las Vegas, earning a bachelors degree in Theatre Arts-Performance/Acting For the Camera.

Over the past decade, I have had the artistic pleasure and good fortune of working on many student and independent film productions. During that time I have worn the hats of producer, director, actor, writer, and editor. Several of the projects I was involved with went on to win awards on the national student film festival circuit, and the first independent film I produced was selected to screen at a major international film festival from among thousands of entries.

Some of what I have learned about filmmaking has been in the lecture hall; more has come purely from the experience of doing. Admittedly, the lessons I learned while actively working on film productions still resonate deeply with me, and no doubt were some of the most expensive! As a product of my combined experiences in film and video work, school, and production-related courses, this book is in many ways the one that I wish I had at the beginning of my career.

1
PRODUCTION BASICS

GETTING STARTED

In its most basic form, a film is essentially a series of shots, comprised of moving images, connected together in a particular order, sequence or set of sequences in a way that *tells a story*.

As we begin our journey into the art of filmmaking, a commitment to putting the story first will be both the foundation and the fuel that drives us throughout this highly personal and creative process. You will need to tell your story in pictures, and no two individuals will interpret the same material in exactly the same way. Therefore, in order to develop a unique style and bring his or her vision to life, a filmmaker must have a solid foundation and understanding of the core principles and basic skills used again and again on all types of productions at every level of the industry. This chapter is designed to illustrate some of the basic shots that will make up the building blocks of your story.

The **Master** or **Establishing Shot** is a continuous shot, or *take*, that captures the primary action or setting of a scene in its entirety (a.k.a. *Long Shot*).

Once the master shot has been established, it will be necessary to shoot **Coverage**. Coverage refers to all of the remaining shots and camera angles needed for the finished product. A **Full Shot** or **Wide Shot** is composed so that it frames the subject's entire body.

A **Medium Shot** is a shot composition usually framing a subject from a point somewhere between the waist and knees up to the top of the head (a.k.a. *Cowboy Shot*). A medium shot may contain multiple subjects as in a *two-shot* or *three-shot*.

A **Medium Close-Up** is a shot composition usually framing a subject from the chest area up (a.k.a. *Bust Shot*).

A **Close-Up** is a shot composition usually framing a subject from the neck and shoulders up to the top of the head.

An **Extreme Close-Up** is framed even tighter than a Close-Up shot, and is often used to isolate a particular object or feature such as the eyes or mouth.

An **Insert** is a shot within a sequence or scene that is usually close-up in orientation and intended to draw the viewer's attention to an object or other piece of visual information that is of particular importance to the story. Some examples might include the timer on a ticking bomb, a photograph, a ransom note, or a hand reaching for a weapon — as shown in the image below.

Depending on the characteristics of a given project, the specific camera angles and coverage needed may vary. When it is time to create your shot list, you need to consider carefully what shot set-ups will be essential to completing the film. Some directors choose to include a "wish list" of extra set-ups in their shot lists that would be nice to have, but are not absolutely necessary. It is more important, however, to focus first on making sure you are getting the shots that you know for sure are going to be needed. Once you have everything you need, if time and circumstance permit, you can then go and get those extra *bonus shots*.

The **Rule of Thirds** is a set of composition guidelines that refers to the imaginary division of the camera frame or screen area into three equal parts, both horizontally and vertically. Picture two horizontal lines dividing the frame into three equal strips going across, and two vertical lines dividing the frame in three equal parts lengthwise, and now see the resulting grid. As a general rule, it is best to frame your subject so that the focal point lands at or near one of the intersections created by these lines.

Also, it is optimal to keep the subject's eyes level with the top third line, with the majority of the open screen space in the direction they are looking. This space in front of the subject is called *nose room* or *look room*. Space between the top of a subject's head and the top of the frame is called *head room*. If a subject is in motion, such as a person running or a moving car, the space in front of the moving object is called *lead room*.

It is more desirable to keep the eyes at the level of the top-third line than it is to maintain head room above the subject. In other words, it is better to "cut off" some of the top of a head than to include it only to have the eyes positioned so low that the subject's head appears to be sinking in the frame.

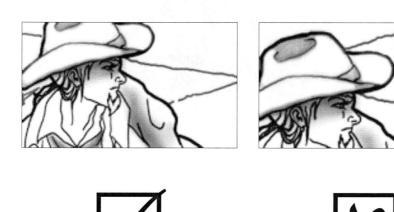

It is also more important to include part of the neck and shoulders in a close up than to get in the entire top of the head. Viewers will readily accept that the top of the head is cut off, as the mind's eye tends to fill in the part that's missing. However, if you frame a close up just below the chin without including any portion of the neck and shoulders, the result is a somewhat freakish effect of a floating head that appears to be severed from its body.

A camera move either upward or downward is called a **Tilt**.

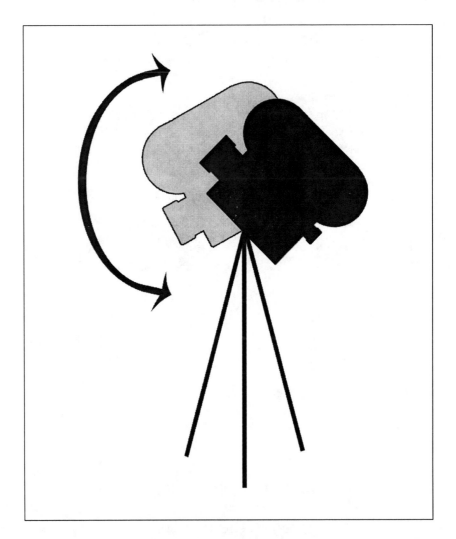

Tilt Up or *Tilt Down*

A camera move from side to side is called a **Pan**.

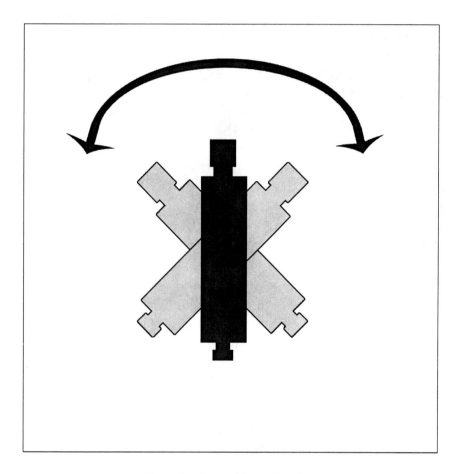

Pan Left or *Pan Right*

CROSSING THE LINE

When shooting coverage of a scene, it is important to maintain a spatial relationship between subjects that is consistent with what was established in the master. The **line of action** is an imaginary division of the staging area that typically runs along the axis on which the principal subjects are placed. Once the *line* is established, it is now a matter of setting up the shots that follow with the camera positioned on the same side of the line as it was in the master. This way, no matter how you frame your subjects or from what angle they are shot, they will always be looking the same direction as they were looking in the master. Thus preserving the continuity of screen direction. This basic convention is also commonly known as the *180-degree rule*. If consecutive shots take place with the camera positioned on opposing sides of this division, it will result in what is known as *crossing the line*. Doing so results in the confusion and disorientation of the viewing audience. Therefore it is rarely done, except for circumstances in which it either cannot be avoided or it is intentionally being done to achieve a particular effect.

One way to visualize the line when choosing camera placement is to imagine that the action of the scene were taking place underneath the hoop area on a basketball court with the two main characters standing facing one another on the boundary line that runs directly beneath the backboard. That way the out of bounds line could represent the line of action. Now you can position the camera anywhere you want to shoot coverage as long as you keep it on the "in-bounds" side of the line. Of course, once one of the characters moves from their original position, a new line of action will be established. Likewise, if a third player enters the scene in progress, new lines will again emerge as a result of the characters' spatial relationship to one another. As the rest of the coverage is shot, subsequent camera positions will now be determined taking into account the proximity of all of the characters being staged in order to preserve continuity of screen direction.

Line of Action

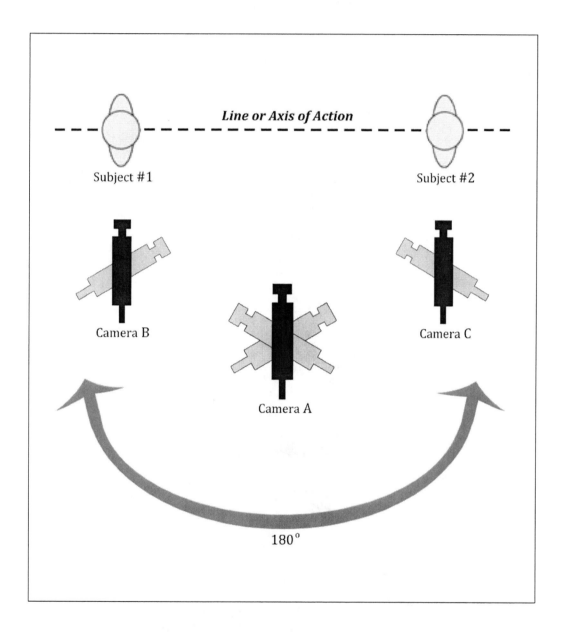

A **dolly shot**/**trucking shot** is a moving shot taken from a camera that is mounted on a wheeled platform called a *dolly* or *truck* that is usually hydraulically powered, and typically rides on rails, or *tracks*, so that the camera can move smoothly and quietly during operation (a.k.a. *follow shot* or *tracking shot*).

Dolly shown with track

Photo courtesy of J.L. FISHER, INC.
Motion Picture and Television Equipment

A **jib arm** is a counterweighted camera mounting system, typically supported by a dolly, tripod or other mounting platform and is used to increase the camera's range of motion.

Jib Arm shown mounted on Dolly

Photo courtesy of J.L. FISHER, INC.
Motion Picture and Television Equipment

A **zoom-in/zoom-out** differs from a dolly/trucking shot in that the changing perspective of "pushing in" or "pulling back" is achieved mechanically inside the camera, either digitally or with the aid of a variable focal length lens. The camera remains in a static position as opposed to a dolly/trucking shot in which the camera is moving. Since the human eye cannot change focal length incrementally like a zoom lens, a zooming shot appears unnatural. These shots are often reserved for the purpose of achieving a special effect or forcing the viewers attention to a particular object or event.

There are distinct differences between a zoom and a dolly shot that should be considered when choosing between the two. A zoom will have the effect of magnifying everything in the frame in equal proportions. A dolly shot will make the object in the foreground larger while changing the size of objects in the background much less as determined by the relative distance between the objects. Therefore, the greater the physical distance between the subject in the foreground and the background, the greater the change in size of just the subject in the foreground that will occur, while the background will appear less affected.

Although certainly not a substitute for a dolly shot, if executed very slowly and smoothly, a zoom can provide a look somewhat similar to a dolly shot if budgetary or logistical circumstances do not allow for a dolly and track. A little old-fashioned ingenuity can go a long way when improvising moving shots. Creative filmmakers will figure out a way to mount a camera on just about anything that rolls in order to approximate the movement of a dolly and track, or perhaps even to achieve a specific look that is intended to be shaky or unstable. Moving shots taken by a skilled operator employing the use of rolling objects such as shopping carts, wheelchairs and garden wagons have been know to produce some highly successful results.

Camera stabilization systems are specially designed mounting devices that are used to facilitate smooth camera operation. Some stabilization systems are compact and lightweight enough to be easily held in one hand, while other models incorporate the use of body harnesses designed to be worn by the camera operator.

Camera Stabilization System

Photo courtesy of GLIDECAM INDUSTRIES, INC.
Camera Stabilization Systems

FOCUS & DEPTH OF FIELD

Focus refers to the sharpness, clarity and distinctness of an image. **Depth of field** refers to the area, or more specifically, the vertical plane of space, in front of the camera in which the objects seen by the camera are in focus.

All of the space between the camera and the subject is known as the **foreground**, while everything behind the subject is called the **background**.

In *Fig 1.1* below, the entire image is in focus including both the subject and background. In *Fig 1.2* illustrates a shallow depth of field in which only the subject is in focus.

Fig 1.1

Fig 1.2

As a general rule, it is usually acceptable to maintain focus for approximately 1/3 of the area in front of the subject, or *foreground*, and 2/3 of the area behind the subject, or *background*. When a shot begins with a subject out of focus, then the focus is pulled to bring that subject into focus, while the background simultaneously goes out — this is commonly called a **rack focus**.

Background IN focus & Subject OUT of focus

Background OUT of focus & Subject IN focus

This operation may also be performed in reverse — beginning with the subject in focus then bringing the background into focus. Meanwhile the subject simultaneously goes out of focus, thus forcing the viewer's attention to the background.

ASPECT RATIO

Aspect ratio refers to the dimensions of an image on screen, determined by how it was shot and arrived at by dividing its width by its height — expressed Width:Height. The aspect ratio used in early films until the mid-1950's was called Academy Aperture, 4:3 (or 1.33:1), and was the same as that of a standard television screen. An aspect ratio of 16:9 (or 1.78:1) is universal for European digital television, as well as modern high-definition widescreen formats. Academy CinemaScope (widescreen movie format) and other anamorphic systems have an aspect ratio of 2.35:1. In the industry, the short form of the word, Scope, is often associated with the use of anamorphic projection or lenses, or in reference to any 2.35:1 or 2.39:1 presentation. Common aspect ratios for modern feature films shot in 35mm are 1.85:1 and 2.39:1. Still photography applications typically use aspect ratios of 4:3 and 3:2. Although this information may sound technical, the purpose for including it here is simple. It is to bring awareness to the different aspect ratios so you will plan your shots in a way that is optimal for whatever format is best suited for the final output of your project.

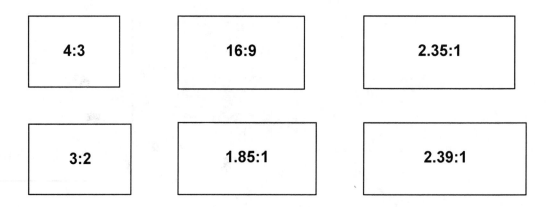

WHITE BALANCE

White balancing is a color balance function that gives the camera a reference to *true white,* so that objects that are white will be captured and recorded accurately. It is important to white balance the camera whenever a significant change in lighting conditions occurs, and especially every time you move between outside and inside locations.

Many video cameras come standard with an *automatic white balance* feature. This function is not always dependable, so if your camera has a manual white balance function, it is strongly suggested that you perform this function before every shoot.

To manually perform a white balance, find the camera's white balance button or switch, then, point the camera at a pure white, relatively non-reflective surface area so that most or the entire viewfinder becomes a white frame. Activate the white balance button and allow the camera to perform the function and hold the setting. Most cameras will indicate on the display when the operation is successful.

MULTIPLE FORMATS — SINGLE PURPOSE

Whether you are shooting on film, video, HD video, tape-less video or any other method of moving image capture, many of the basic principles have remained relatively constant over the history of motion picture photography. The goal of this chapter has been to provide a practical understanding of the fundamental principles and technical aspects of moving image capture related to camera operation and shot composition, regardless of the medium.

CHAPTER SUMMARY

- Study shots used in television and film and observe the framing conventions being used.

- Use the Rule of Thirds as a guide when composing shots.

- Practice performing a zoom vs. a dolly shot and observe the way they affect the perspective of the image differently.

- When planning shot set-ups, always give priority to the camera angles you cannot do without.

- Remember to white-balance the camera:

  o   Before every shoot.

  o   Every time lighting conditions change.

  o   Whenever moving between indoors and outdoors.

2

THE SCRIPT

A **script** is the written text of a filmed production that details the story and its setting, the sequence of events, and the actions and dialogue of the actors.

As the blueprint for your project, the script deserves the same attention to detail that would be required if you were an architect drafting plans for the construction of a building. No matter the scale of the project, a well-crafted script contains the code that will guide everyone involved in bringing the project, the vision, and ultimately the message to life.

Once you have decided on the overall concept of your particular script or project idea, there are still some important questions you will need to address.

What is the intended message? First and foremost, you must be clear on what it is you are trying to say. What kind of impact do you expect to have on the viewer, and what type of emotional response do you want to evoke with your message? This central theme will be the driving force that will shape all of the events in the story.

Who is your target audience? Understanding the demographic to which your project is intended to appeal is crucial and will have a great deal of impact on all aspects of the production. A product or message designed to reach 18-35 year old males, for example, will naturally be crafted much differently than one meant to target a viewing audience of single moms or persons 55 and older.

Through what medium will your work be distributed and/or viewed? This will also need to be given careful consideration from the very beginning stages of pre-production.

FILMMAKING IS STORYTELLING!

There cannot be enough emphasis placed on the importance of serving the story when approaching a film or video project. After all, it is the story that will captivate the viewer and elicit an emotional response. Making the audience *feel* something is the principal goal of the craft.

First, you must identify what category your production falls into. Be clear on what particular story your piece is going to tell. Are you producing a short story or feature length narrative, a commercial advertisement for television or the internet, a news program or electronic news gathering (ENG) out in the field, a music video, a documentary, a corporate training or safety video, special event videography, reality programming, or perhaps some hybrid visual medium of your own invention?

Regardless of the particular format, one thing that has changed little over the history of filmmaking is the use of basic story structure consisting of a clearly identifiable *beginning, middle* and *end*. Narrative pieces of any length will have a beginning, or *setup*, that serves to introduce the central characters and conflict; followed by a middle section, or *conflict*, with confrontations and developing complications that will lead to a *climax;* and finally an end, or *resolution*, that concludes the piece and accounts for the remainder of the story. The elements of this standard cinematic three-act structure appear in most films, and are useful tools for you to use in practicing script analysis.

Cinematic Three-Act Structure

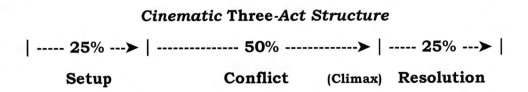

| ----- 25% ---➤ | --------------- 50% -------------➤ | ----- 25% ---➤ |

Setup   **Conflict**   (Climax) **Resolution**

NARRATIVE WRITING

Telling a story is at the very core of the narrative writing process. Narrative works are often adapted into motion pictures resulting in a highly effective medium through which the viewer can experience the story. As with all storytelling, doing this requires the introduction and development of three essential elements that will be the building blocks of the story structure.

Character — *Who* is the story about?

Setting — *Where* and *When* does the story take place?

Plot — *What* are the sequence of events? *Why* do they occur? and *How* does it all play out?

DOCUMENTARIES

Documentary filmmaking often involves the exploration of subject matter that is political, historical, or socially significant in some way. It is not unusual for a documentary piece to contain a variety of source footage with completely different looks. It may, for example, contain a combination of elements like news broadcast clips, historic film footage, taped interviews that are either planned or impromptu, or still photos with narration over top. This type of programming tends to have more of a gritty feel to it. Therefore, the convention of cutting together images that originate from different sources and are of varying levels of picture quality has come to be expected from this genre and is readily accepted by the documentary viewing audience. Structurally, the documentary typically requires the filmmaker to 1) tell viewers what you are going to tell them, 2) tell them what you are telling them, and 3) tell them what you told them. Although the length of these parts may or may not adhere to the cinematic structure as described on the previous page, successful documentaries will also have a clearly identifiable beginning, middle and end.

COMMERCIALS

Commercial scripts, whether for filmed media or radio, typically are no more than one or two pages in length and are called **copy**. These scripts will also have a beginning, middle and end. Of course, the primary goal here is to focus on the product or service being advertised. Although there is plenty of room for individual creativity and technical flair when constructing an effective advertisement, it is important to never lose sight of the intended message. That message, of course, is the perceived value of the particular product or service being offered. If the product is an object such as a food item or cleaning product, the filmed specimen that appears in the commercial is called the *hero product*. Pay special attention to details when dealing with the hero item in terms of screen time, screen placement, and the inflection of an actor or announcer's voice when saying the product name. Some of the most successful advertising campaigns are designed so that it is difficult to determine what the product or service is until the very end of the commercial. When executed effectively, curiosity and suspense build until the product or service is finally revealed, leaving a lasting impression on the viewer. The net effect should be a synergistic one that focuses the viewer's attention on the product or service in a way that makes it both appealing and necessary to purchase.

WEB VIDEOS

We are becoming increasingly more accustomed to viewing news, entertainment, and advertising on the Internet. When writing and producing content intended for web viewing, there are a couple of things to consider. Attention spans of typical web-based audience members tend to be short. Therefore it is generally a good practice to get to the point, keep up the pace, and stick to shorter running times. Also keep in mind that many people will be seeing your video on a very small screen or viewing area, such as a mobile phone or other portable device.

It is wise to be planning during the writing process for how that might influence the way a particular scene or sequence will need to be shot.

BRAINSTORMING

Brainstorming is a practice that is unique to each individual. It does not matter what particular series of steps you follow or technique you use. What *is* important is that you develop a system that works for you consistently, and that you experiment with whatever method gets your creative juices flowing and helps you cultivate workable ideas. If you are working with a writing partner or a team of writers, you may agree to brainstorm individually and then come together to present your ideas. Or, it may work best to schedule a production meeting dedicated to script development and explore the brainstorming process collectively. Again, there is no right or wrong way to approach the creative process. It is up to you to determine the system that works best for you, and best serves the production.

BRAINSTORMING EXERCISE

These types of creative writing exercises should be written by hand. In the brainstorming exercise the goal is to explore a central idea or theme in a way that generates a myriad of related ideas, themes and subject matter. You might wish to start by simply writing down your central topic or theme in the center of a blank piece of paper. Next, in the space surrounding your topic, begin jotting down any related topics, themes or ideas that come to mind. Do not attempt to out-think the process by over-analyzing it! Just keep the pencil moving until you have written down every word, idea or phrase related to your central theme that you can think of. Then see if you can squeeze out a few more.

Once you have collected a good bit of ammunition, you can start to refine the process by selecting key words and phrases that will help unify your thoughts into a clearly defined idea or message. This is the story you will tell.

FREEWRITING

Freewriting is a common literary exercise used by writers in order to access a free-flowing stream of consciousness without having to be concerned with spelling, grammar, or sentence structure. In fact, letting the process be interrupted by thoughts of these things actually hinders the exercise. Freewriting can be a great way to work through frustrating spells of "writer's block", as well as an effective tool for uncovering thoughts and ideas that may be buried deep within the unconscious mind.

FREEWRITING EXCERCISE

Start by setting aside time and choose an environment that is comfortable to write in. Make a commitment to freewrite for a set amount of time, say perhaps 5 or 7 minutes to start. The single most important aspect of the exercise is to keep writing continuously for the entire time without stopping. It might even be helpful to set a timer. Now to begin the exercise simply start writing whatever comes to mind. Do not allow the pen or pencil to stop moving for any reason, even if you find yourself repeating words or feel as if what you are writing is not making any sense. Just keep writing. As simple as the exercise might seem, the most difficult part for most writers is to turn off their own inner critic that will want to analyze, criticize, and correct everything as it is being written down. Many people find that writing with a pen or pencil tends to foster a higher degree of creativity than using a computer-based word processor. It might be a good idea to try several different methods in order to see what works best for you.

SCREENWRITING FORMAT

There are several quality screenwriting software applications available that will automatically format your script to industry standard specifications. However, if your budget does not allow for screenwriting software, you can always prepare your script with a conventional word processing application by simply setting the tabs for the different elements of the scripted page.

You can closely emulate the format of most popular screenwriting programs and achieve a professional-looking result by setting up your page using these guidelines:

Start by setting the left margin at 1.5 inches, set both the top and bottom margins at .75 inches, and set the right margin at .5 inches. The reason for the wide left margin is because scripts are usually bound with a three-hole punch and brads. This eats up space on the left of the page and would otherwise make it difficult to see all of the text.

From the fonts menu, you will want to choose 12-point "Courier" or "Courier New". These tend to be closest to [if not the actual] font styles used by most of the popular script writing software programs.

A *character name* is placed five tabs in from the left margin and is in all caps, as in "STEVEN" for example. A character's name also appears in all caps the first time they are introduced in the script.

Dialogue will begin ten spaces, or two tabs in from the left margin, and should end ten spaces or two tabs from the right margin. A parenthetical dialogue direction would appear three tabs in, on the line between the character's name and the dialogue.

If a character's voice is heard while they are out of the camera's range of view or **Off-Screen**, the abbreviation **(O.S.)** is used. If a character's voice is heard but he is never seen, such as a narrator, it is called a **Voice-Over** and the abbreviation **(V.O.)** is used.

A voice-over may also be used to convey the thoughts taking place or the voice being "heard" within the character's head, sometimes referred to as *internal dialogue.*

Lines describing the *action* of the scene begin at the left margin.

Shot headings, also called "slug lines" begin at the left margin and appear in all caps. Shot headings indicate the location, time of day, and whether the scene occurs indoors or outside. The abbreviations INT. and EXT. are used to indicate interior or exterior shots.

It is common practice to skip a space so that there will be two blank lines between the end of one scene and a new shot heading.

Transitions are aligned against the right margin, as in...

                                                            CUT TO:

```
FADE IN:


INT. CLASSROOM -- DAY


                    STEVEN
               (authoritatively)
          I guess you could say a typical
          page of script in screenplay format
          would look something like this…


Steven quickly exits the classroom, leaving
the students to gaze around the room at one
another.


                    STEVEN (O.S.)
          Even though you guys can't see me,
          I know that you can definitely still
          hear my voice!


                                        CUT TO:


EXT. SOME OTHER LOCATION -- EVENING
```

STORYBOARDING

A **storyboard** is a visual representation, typically in the form of multiple illustrations, each of which captures the essence of the primary images that will tell the story, usually in chronological order. When setting out to create your storyboard, a good place to start is to simply think in terms of how your story would be depicted in a comic strip or graphic novel format. Sketches are used to illustrate the individual beats that make up the plot. Often these sketches may include arrows or other methods of notation indicating specific camera angles and movement. An example of a storyboard can be seen on the next page.

In addition to a traditional storyboard rendering, you might want to consider creating a *digital storyboard* by taking still photos at the actual locations you are planning to shoot, if possible. You can then arrange the photos on your computer and begin to get a picture of how the scenes might look once they are strung together in sequence.

CREATING A SHOT LIST

At some point during pre-production, a director will compose a **shot list**. This is a list of all the shots needed from every camera angle for every scene of a day's shooting schedule. Some directors develop a detailed shot list over the course of several weeks leading up to the shoot, while some prefer to put a shot list together on the night before or even the morning of the first day of shooting. A shot list should include the scene numbers or headings in the order they are to be shot, the camera angle of each set-up, as well as indication of camera movements or other special instructions.

STORYBOARD

Project: COWBOY WALKING

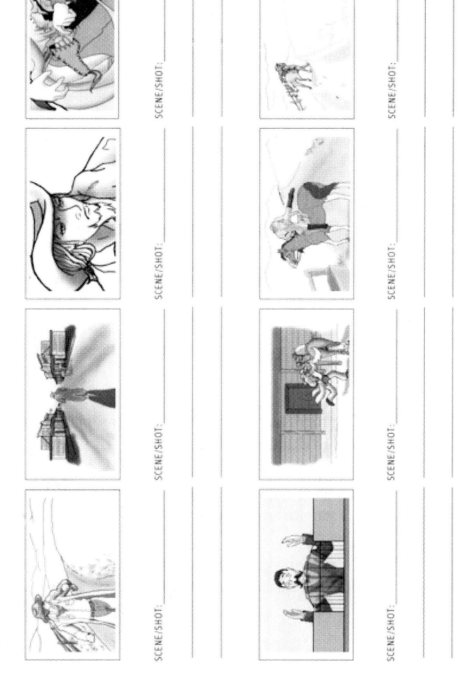

SCENE/SHOT:

SCENE/SHOT:

SCENE/SHOT:

SCENE/SHOT:

SCENE/SHOT:

SCENE/SHOT:

SCENE/SHOT:

SCENE/SHOT:

Directors often work closely with an assistant director in preparing a shot list. A good assistant director is going to make it his or her business to be aware of the logistical challenges and other potential pitfalls associated with the day's shooting schedule, and therefore will often have a good idea of what order would be most efficient to set up the shots.

Abbreviations for some common camera angles are:

LS – *Long Shot,* WS or FS – *Wide* or *Full Shot,* MS – *Medium Shot,* MCU – *Medium Close-Up,* CU – *Close-Up,* ECU – *Extreme Close-Up,* INS – *Insert.*

CHAPTER SUMMARY

- ✍ Always be clear on what your message is and be aware of your target audience.

- ✍ Focus on a clearly distinguishable beginning, middle and end.

- ✍ Commercial copy is designed in order to emphasize the product or service for sale.

- ✍ Become familiar with and adhere to industry standard screenwriting formats.

- ✍ Storyboard your project and make arrangements to take digital photos of locations if possible.

3
PRE-PRODUCTION

Pre-production includes all components of the filmmaking process that take place from the inception of a project up to the first day of principal photography. This includes but is not limited to elements such as overall concept and story development, screenwriting, budgeting, scheduling, casting, location scouting, permits, rehearsal, set design, props and equipment checks. Although your client/audience will have no idea how much time and effort you put into pre-production, the results of your labor and attention to detail during this critical process will definitely show in your final product.

Production **budgeting** involves preparing a detailed breakdown of the expenses associated with the making of a film. Production-related expenses are typically divided into two major categories. **Above the line costs** represent expenses associated with creative personnel such as producer(s), director, writer(s) and lead actors. **Below the line costs** refer to all expenses in the budget of a film project other than the *above-the-line costs*, such as remaining cast, crew, props, equipment rental, and craft services.

Production **scheduling** entails setting up the timeline for making a film as well as mapping out the logistical elements of the filming. A shooting schedule should plan for the most efficient use of available time and resources, and take into account the best way to handle location changes and company moves. Most production budgeting and scheduling is done with the aid of specially designed budgeting and scheduling software.

By the time you complete pre-production you will need to have prepared a **Shooting script**. That is a final version of a script with scenes numbered and arranged in the order they are to be shot. This way the scenes will appear in the same sequence as in the shooting schedule.

Breakdown sheets are often used to list the necessary elements of a production. Breakdown sheets are often prepared for individual scenes, but they may also be based on the shooting schedule for a particular day or set of days. Breakdowns contain information such as cast, extras, props, music, sound effects, vehicles, animals and special effects. There are many budgeting and scheduling software applications on the market designed to track script elements and generate breakdown sheets and other production forms. Such programs do enhance the efficiency of a production, but you can also create forms of your own. A breakdown sheet has been included in the production forms at the back of this book.

Before going out to shoot a project you will first need to obtain a **film permit**. It is necessary to begin the application process for a permit as soon as you have determined the tentative date(s) and location(s) of the shoot. Do not assume that you can fax the application and related paperwork to your local film office a few days before you intend to start shooting and they will approve your request in time for your first day of production. Although this is certainly possible, I can tell you from personal experience that it simply does not always work out, so it is best to plan ahead. Another commonly overlooked element is the matter of **production insurance**. This is an insurance policy that provides coverage designed to accommodate the specific needs of a film or video production. Typical production insurance policies includes:

- o Liability coverage (insurance for personal injury and property damage claims).

- o Miscellaneous equipment coverage (insurance for damage to camera, sound, lighting and other production-related equipment).

- o Errors and omissions coverage (insurance for actions related to civil matters such as claims of slander, plagiarism or unauthorized use of the likeness and image of a person, place or product).

Many film offices will not issue permits without first seeing proof of production insurance. If you are enrolled in a film or video production class at an educational institution, your school may already carry a blanket production insurance policy that covers student film crews shooting class-related projects. This is one of the benefits of being a student filmmaker. Do not, however, assume that your school has such a policy before you go out and shoot. Check with your instructor and/or the department chair to find out for sure. If such a policy is in place, be sure to get a copy of the current certificate of insurance for your files. This will also prove helpful in gaining the confidence of business and property owners when it comes time to approach them about shooting at their location.

Consult your state or local film office in order to find out what the insurance requirements are in terms of coverage limits to make sure that your policy is adequate. You will usually be required to show proof of production insurance by providing a copy of the insurance certificates, or *certs*, as part of the film permit application process. When shopping for production insurance, it is much more cost effective to purchase a policy for the entire year instead of purchasing coverage for a few days at a time every time you go out and shoot a project.

Many novice filmmakers take pride in less refined tactics like a "run and gun" shooting style without regard for such details as film permits, location releases, and insurance. Bucking the system only opens you up to risking things such as unwanted confrontation with local authorities or being named in a lawsuit. If you are serious about this craft, it is a sound practice to start forming good habits early and get accustomed to working within the system. There is nothing cool about having a production held up or possibly even shut down entirely because nobody bothered to secure a film permit, releases and proof of insurance!

CHAPTER SUMMARY

✎   Careful attention to detail in the early phases of pre-production will be rewarded greatly later on.

✎   Prepare a production budget and shooting schedule, complete with breakdowns, regardless of the size of the project.

✎   Check to see if your school provides production insurance or look into a policy of your own.

✎   Begin the permit application process as soon as you have determined your tentative shooting dates and locations.

✎   Get familiar with your local film offices and play by the rules.

4

CREW UP ALREADY!

Make no mistake about it — filmmaking is by all means a team sport. Just imagine a football squad putting eleven quarterbacks on the field. All the opposing team would have to do is just sit back and watch as the whole mess of quarterbacks fight over who is going to throw the ball. The same could be said for the members of a film crew. Each job title has a specific function and set of duties inherent to that position, and not everyone can be directing at the same time. When all of the members of a film crew are working together in a collaborative effort, a synergy occurs that results in a final product where the whole is definitely greater than the sum of its parts. Here are some of the essential players that make up a film or video production unit and crew.

The **Producer** is the individual in charge of overseeing the production of a film project. There may be one or many producers on any given production. It is typically the producer who acquires the script or story idea, secures funding for the project, and hires the creative personnel that will make up the production team. A good producer must have the ability to multitask, as well as possess a working knowledge of the duties inherent to every other position on the crew being assembled.

The **Director** is the person responsible for overseeing all of the creative aspects of a film production. A director will interpret the script in order to turn it into a finished project, while supervising the technical crews as well as directing and shaping performances of the actors. Although a director is by nature a creative artist, a vast majority of one's success at this position depends on his or her communication skills. All of the brilliance and grandeur of whatever it is you have worked up in your head will be for naught if you are unable to effectively communicate your vision to the cast and crew members in a way that they not only understand, but become motivated to support you in seeing it to fruition.

As the director, it is imperative to know exactly what you want at all times. According to director De Veau Dunn, "A good director plans his day down to every scene, but I've learned that a great director plans his day down to every shot." A great deal of preparation when planning your shots will give you a increased confidence in what you are doing on the set. This will result in others also having confidence in your decision-making process, which will help maintain a unified environment while carrying out the vision of the project.

The **Assistant Director (AD)** is the person who aids the director in the production process. Some of the duties of the AD include preparation of the shooting schedule and call sheets, tending to logistical elements, accounting for the presence of cast and crew members, tracking progress throughout the shooting day, maintaining order and efficiency of the workflow on the set, and rehearsing actors and directing extras. This may sound like a great deal of work and responsibility and for good reason... it is! A successful AD knows this and dares not take the importance of the position lightly. It is often necessary for the AD to bark orders on the set in order to keep the shooting schedule on track and ensure that the production will *make its day*, meaning to get all the shots that were scheduled for that day of shooting. Of all of the duties inherent to the AD's job description, being the most liked person on the set is certainly not one of them.

The **Director of Photography (DP)** is the person responsible for the mechanical aspects of camera placement, movement, operation and lighting exposure. Depending on the nature of the production, the DP may or may not be the person operating the camera. If a project requires more than one camera during production, an additional **Camera Operator** (or operators) may be necessary. This individual will be responsible for operating a camera under the direction of the director and/or the director of photography. On most small productions, the DP and camera operator are likely to be the same person.

It is the job of the **Production Designer** to visualize and create the overall look of a film project. These individuals work closely with the director, DP, and other artistic and technical personnel in order to make decisions regarding visual elements of a production such as set design, lighting, props, wardrobe and makeup.

An **Art Director** works closely with and under the direction of the production designer to help carry out their vision. This individual will be largely responsible for the overall appearance and feel of the set, and is involved with all of the aesthetic details from the selection of construction materials and set dressings to prop placement.

A **Set Designer** is an individual who designs and prepares blueprints and mechanical drawings in order to illustrate in detail the technical elements associated with a set's construction.

A **Set Decorator** is the person in charge of designing, overseeing and setting up the artistic elements of a film set. On larger productions, the set decorator may have a team of *set dressers* responsible for setting up and maintaining the set's appearance.

A **Gaffer**, or head electrician, is the person responsible for the placement and operation of lighting instruments and fixtures, under the direction of the DP.

A **Grip** is a member of the crew responsible for multiple jobs such as setting up camera cranes, laying dolly tracks, moving props or scenery pieces, and moving and maintaining any other equipment that may be in use on the set. The **Key Grip** is the head grip in charge of coordinating the efforts of all grips on the crew, working under the direction of the gaffer. The key grip's main assistant or "right-hand" person is called the **Best Boy Grip**.

Production Assistant is the title given to individuals who will perform a wide variety of functions and tasks on a project, such as getting releases signed, running errands, filing paperwork etc.

A **Script Supervisor** is the person who monitors the internal continuity of a film through careful observation and notation of action, location, wardrobe, props, hair and makeup etc., so that these elements can be recreated and will be consistent throughout filming. Additionally, the script supervisor monitors and keeps a record of the daily progress of a film production.

A **Makeup Artist** is an individual trained in the application and use of makeup specifically for TV and film production. There can be a significant difference between commonly available commercial cosmetics and the products and application techniques used in film makeup. That said, it is well worth it to employ the services of a professional makeup artist whenever possible.

A **Still Photographer** is an individual hired for the purpose of capturing still images in order to document elements of the production taking place both on set and behind the scenes. Still photographs of your production will prove to be valuable tools with several important functions. Ranging from tracking continuity to being used in order to promote the finished project.

CHAPTER SUMMARY

- Filmmaking is a team sport!

- Successful directors typically have exceptional communication skills.

- Be ready to wear several different hats and perform multiple functions when working on a small film crew.

- Much of a director's confidence on the set comes from careful preparation, so always be prepared!

5
LOCATION

Location can be defined as an existing place to which a film company or crew travels in order to shoot some or all of a production. Just as in real estate, the function of location in the production process is paramount. There is rarely a more effective way of achieving the overall mood of the image you want to project, or add *production value* to your project, than by selecting the right location.

LOCATION SCOUTING

Location scouting is the process of going out to look at potential locations to shoot your production. When scouting for locations, always take pictures or even document on video. This way you can study the location scouting photos and footage in order to look for elements that you might not have noticed during the physical location scout, and perhaps even incorporate them in a digital storyboard. It will also serve you well to be able to show these images to your department heads when it is time to discuss visual elements such as lighting and set design.

A **set** refers to the physical environment in which the filmed action takes place. Sets may be interior or exterior locales, and may consist of artificially manufactured places (that have been modified from existing locations) or in some cases are constructed entirely from scratch solely for purposes of the production.

A **soundstage** is a spacious, enclosed space or building in a studio facility dedicated for use in film productions that provides a great deal of control over environmental factors such as sound, lighting, climate and set security.

PRIVATE PROPERTY and BUSINESSES

Do not be afraid to approach independently owned and operated businesses such as local restaurants or retail shops to inquire about filming there. Many business owners would be happy to allow you to use their location for filming, at no cost to you, simply in exchange for special thanks to them and/or the name of their business in the end credits. Possibly even a complimentary screening of the finished project. There are also the obvious added benefits of the free advertising they will enjoy if the name of their business or product ends up being shown in the completed film, provided of course that they are not in any way being portrayed in a negative light. If you are planning to shoot at a privately owned location such as a residence or business, you will need to obtain a **location release** from the property owner or authorized agent of the property. This is a signed agreement giving you permission to use the image and likeness of the location in the making of your film or video project.

GREEN SCREENING

A **green screen** (or **blue screen)** is a monochromatic background that can easily be replaced with other images in post-production. This enables a scene to be shot in a studio facility and then made to appear as if it takes place at some other location.

A skilled editor is capable of seamlessly placing a live action scene shot in front of a green screen against a backdrop of an exotic far away location, or even in a fantastical world that is entirely computer generated. This technique is not only great for generating special effects shots, but is also another great opportunity to add maximum production value to a project while keeping costs down.

SCOUT, SELECT, and SECURE *GREAT* LOCATIONS

One of the best ways to give your production an *expensive look* without destroying the budget is to become proficient at choosing great locations. What makes for great locations? Preferably ones that can be secured for little or no money, and that will require minimal set dressing and other modifications in order to prepare for shooting a given project.

When considering potential locations for your project, you will want to determine to what degree the places you are visiting already appear to be in a *camera-ready* state. In order to do so you might start by asking the following questions. Does the prospective location already have interesting colors and textures, or is it plain and boring to look at? For interior scenes, is there already an adequate amount of appropriate set dressing in place, or will the location require a great deal of potentially costly and time consuming re-decorating in order to achieve a specific look? For exterior scenes, are there any issues involving noise, unusual lighting conditions or other particular environmental factors that might present challenges for the technical departments? Making detailed notes about these and other observations pertaining to the particular needs of your production will be valuable when it comes time to narrow down your location choices and make the final selections.

From a producer's perspective, a camera-ready location that looks great, can be secured for free (or very little money), and is well suited for the needs of the production is always desirable. Locations that fit all of these criteria are considered to be "production friendly", and will pay off big when it comes time to shoot as well as adding production value to the overall look of the production. Locations that are easily secured, cost-effective, and have a high degree of camera-readiness tend to make for very happy producers.

MINDING THE DETAILS

As briefly mentioned in the last section, an extremely important consideration of location scouting is taking into account and making notes about logistical concerns. Always pay careful attention to circumstances that may impede your ability to record clean sound, such as low-flying aircraft or the noisy hum of a nearby freeway. Be aware of how these and other environmental characteristics of a potential location could affect the production should you decide to shoot there. Observe nearby traffic patterns of automobiles and pedestrians. Will the normal flow of vehicle and/or foot traffic be interrupted as a result of the production? Is there potential for issues of crowd control? If so, then you will have to assess the possible need for the presence of private security or police officers on location.

Make sure the location will be easily accessible to cast, crew and production vehicles. See to it that there will be adequate parking available on all of the shooting days. Also, make note of the ready availability of accommodations such as access to public restrooms and shelter from adverse weather conditions that may occur unexpectedly. Taking the time to iron out these types of details during location scouting and throughout the remainder of the pre-production phase is crucial.

CHAPTER SUMMARY

- Careful selection of locations can add a great deal of production value to a project.

- Make sure chosen locations are accessible and can accommodate parking for the entire cast and crew.

- Always take pictures while scouting locations.

- Approach local merchants who might be happy to let you film at their business.

- Pay specific attention to circumstances that will impede your ability to record clean sound such as low flying aircraft or the noisy hum of a nearby freeway

6

CASTING

Casting is the process of selecting and hiring actors to appear in a production. An **actor** is any performer (male, female or animal) that appears in a film production. An individual in charge of supervising animal actors on the set is called the **Animal Handler** or **Animal Wrangler**.

Just how important is good casting to the success of a film project? To put it bluntly, casting is everything. "Wait a minute, didn't you just say location was everything?" Not exactly, I believe I said location was paramount. Casting, on the other hand, is *everything*! Casting can, and will, make or break your production. As producer and/or director, whether you come out looking like a creative genius or an absolute buffoon will depend largely on the performances of the actors *you* selected during the casting process. After all, it is with the actors [and the portrayal of their characters] that the viewers must identify. It is the actors who will ultimately tell the story.

A **personal release** is a signed agreement that gives permission for you to use a person's image and likeness (including their recorded voice) in the making and future promotion of your film or video project. If at all possible, it is highly recommended that you videotape your auditions so that you can review the playback at a later time. If you are going to be filming actors at an audition, be sure to have them sign a personal release immediately after they have checked in, and before the recorded portion of the audition begins.

CASTING NOTICES

There are several places you may be able to post casting notices locally that will typically cost very little or nothing at all, such as:

☆   Student union bulletin boards.

☆   Theatre/Film department bulletin boards.

☆   Free classifieds (Internet or Printed Periodical).

☆   Actors alliance local chapter or website.

Below is an example of a casting notice that might appear in the Internet classifieds or on an acting network bulletin board:

Non-Union Television Commercial

NOW CASTING for the following speaking and non-speaking roles:

MUSCLE GUY, 20's all-American jock stereotype. COLLEGE GIRL, 18-22, attractive, brainy confidence. GRUMPY OLD MAN, 60+, balding or grey hair, rough voice. EXTRAS, male / female college students.

There is pay for principal roles. Copy and meals provided. Please submit headshot/resume via email and be sure to include the role(s) you are submitting for in the subject line. Auditions are by appointment only. Selected individuals will be notified by email along with time and location. Please come prepared to read if you are auditioning for a speaking role.

Thanks and good luck!

AT THE AUDITION

Upon arrival at the audition location, the first thing your actors will do is put their names on a master *sign-in sheet*, along with the time they arrived and perhaps any other information you wish to include, such as union affiliations or agency representation. If you need more detailed personal information, as in physical statistics and/or clothing sizes, you should prepare a separate form called a *size card* to be filled out by each actor individually.

Have a production assistant be responsible for duties such as greeting actors upon arrival, having them sign in, and getting them started on their personal release forms and any other necessary paperwork. As the actors are checking in and filling out their size cards, the production assistant should also be taking digital photos of each actor. If you are the one directing the casting session, having other team members taking care of these important elements will free up your concentration so that you can focus on doing your job; finding the right actors for the roles.

One way to conduct an audition is by having the actors read a scene from the actual script you are shooting. These scenes or pages pulled from the script are called **sides**. If there is dialogue with another character involved, you can have another actor read the other part off-camera, have an assistant read or even read with them yourself.

Another way to hold auditions is to simply provide actors with a scenario to play out and have them improvise a character. Improv auditions are a great way to get an idea of a performer's ability to adapt to a given situation and quickly draw upon their own unique interpretation and characterization of the material. This also provides a blank slate for the actor's creativity that may yield particular inspiration for an approach to the scene work you otherwise might not have envisioned.

Some auditions are more dependent on the particular appearance of the actor and may require no more than having them simply say his/her name for the camera, then turn to profile each side. If you wish to see more of the actor's personality, simply ask them to tell you a little about themselves, or prompt them to talk about anything, like what they did last weekend, what was their most embarrassing moment, or something along those lines.

Some desirable traits in actors that you should be looking for at the audition are the willingness to make choices and commit to them as well as ability to take direction. Even if an actor gives a great reading the first time through, do not hesitate to ask them to do it another way. Likewise, do not simply count someone out because his or her initial read went in a completely opposite direction than your own personal interpretation. Simply respect the fact that they made a strong choice, and ask them to try it differently, perhaps offering a single, simple bit of specific direction to see what they do with it.

Never bombard an actor with an overwhelming array of acting suggestions and director's notes all at once. If you do, chances are good that they will only remember the last thing you said anyway. That is, of course, if they remember anything at all and you have not already managed to shut them down completely.

On large-scale productions or when starting with a significant number of actors, it is common to narrow the search after the initial round of auditions by holding **callbacks**. These are subsequent audition(s) an actor has been invited to at the request of the director or producer(s). Callbacks give you the opportunity to take another look at select actors in order to make a better-informed decision as to who will be best for the role. It is also an opportunity to match up different combinations of actors that you envision might work well with one another and have them read scenes together.

Remember, when it comes to casting it is always important to remain open-minded. Although you might feel as if you already have the perfect image in your mind's eye of the ideal actor for the role, the truth is you might not really be sure exactly who or what it is you are looking for until you see it. So it is best to remain open-minded. It is also important to make the actors feel as comfortable as possible and you should always be sure to conduct yourself in a professional manner at all times.

CHAPTER SUMMARY

Casting can make or break your production.

Take advantage of free advertising outlets to place casting notices.

At the audition, have actors try things a different way, and look for actors who make strong choices.

Get a personal release signed *before* filming actors at an audition.

Remain open-minded and always be professional.

7

LIGHTING

Lighting is one of the most important elements of motion picture photography. Acquiring a working knowledge of the basic technical aspects of proper lighting technique for film and video is one of the most effective ways to achieve the desired look of any production. Production lighting design is a discipline that is both highly technical and artistic at the same time. A good producer knows this and will strive to bring on a head electrician skilled in both areas and has a proven track record of successfully balancing the two.

OUTDOOR LIGHTING

A great deal of video shooting can be done outdoors simply by utilizing the naturally occurring available light. However, you should not underestimate the importance of being aware of the actual amount and quality of light present while shooting. In situations when you are relying on shooting almost exclusively with the available daylight, you must become adept at making adjustments to the changes in lighting conditions that will inevitably occur throughout the day, as well as skilled in ways to bounce, control, and otherwise manipulate your light source.

It is important to pay particular attention to getting ample light on the faces of your subjects, especially when you are dealing with shadowing in and around the eye socket areas. Bouncing some of the available light onto the subject's face will help eliminate dark circles that result from shadowing while adding sparkle to the eyes. Just be aware that failure to light the eyes may result in a dull, lifeless look that can deaden the actor's on-screen appearance in a way that may or may not best serve your shot, and this should be taken into consideration depending on what type of look you want to achieve.

A **reflector board** may be used as a secondary light source to "bounce" light onto a subject. Typically, silver reflector material will result in a hard white light, and light reflected from gold material will be of a softer tone. If you do not have access to a professional-grade light reflector kit, a piece of white foam core (available for a few bucks at an art supply store) will work well in many instances. Reflector boards are especially useful when you are shooting outside at a remote location without a light kit.

CAMERA FILTERS

There are a wide variety of filters available for all types of shooting conditions. Some filters may be attached directly to the lens housing, while others are designed for use with a **matte box**. A matte box is a square-shaped attachment that is mounted around the camera's lens housing. These types of camera accessories are commonly supported by some variation of a *rail system*. Slots designed to hold filters are built into the matte box, making it easy to switch filters. Further study of cinematography will cover more types of filters and explain their use in greater detail. Two common types of filters with which you should be familiar are discussed here.

If there is too much available light, you may choose to use a **neutral density filter**. Neutral density filters will block some of the light from entering the camera without affecting the color profile of the image. Most pro-sumer and professional grade video cameras have ND functions built into their onboard circuitry.

A **polarizing filter** is capable of selectively removing excessive amounts of light. There are a variety of other specialty filters capable of achieving various looks at the time of image capture. However, it is now more common to add many of these effects as well as perform functions of color-correction in post-production with the use of specialized editing software applications.

PRACTICAL vs. PROFESSIONAL LIGHTING

Practical lighting refers to the use of light sources that are inherent to the scene and as they occur in the real world, such as a household light fixture or a street lamp. *Professional lighting instruments* are specially designed for the purpose of lighting sets. Depending on the needs of a particular scene, professional lighting instruments may be used to enhance, or even entirely provide, the light that appears to be coming from a practical fixture.

Shooting with film typically requires considerably more light to achieve proper exposure than digital video cameras require in converting and recording images. Therefore, shooting digital video often has advantages when working in low-light conditions or with limited access to professional lighting equipment.

Bounce light is a secondary light source achieved by reflecting light from a primary light source off another surface, like a wall or ceiling, and redirected onto a subject or scene.

Color temperature refers to the specific hue (or color) of a given light source, measured in Degrees Kelvin. 3200K is a standard reference point for indoor color balance, while 5600K is common for outdoor (daylight) color balance. Although these temperatures are a basis for color balance with reference to a film stock or video camera, the exact color temperature of a given light source will vary depending on the type of lighting instrument (indoors) or time of day and weather conditions (outdoors). You must pay close attention to circumstances where lights with different color temperatures are mixed, and might cause undesired results. One example is the strong blue cast that occurs on video recordings when sunlight comes in through a window and combines with light from other sources like indoor practical or fluorescent lighting fixtures.

LED LIGHTS

Professional grade **LED (light emitting diode)** instruments are becoming increasingly popular in production lighting applications. These are extremely versatile, durable, energy efficient lights that generate much less heat than fixtures using traditional lamps. As advancements in this technology continue, more applications will emerge and the cost of LED instruments is likely to go down.

3-POINT LIGHTING TECHNIQUE

Standard 3-point lighting technique consists of the following:

A **Key light** is the primary light source used to illuminate the scene and has the greatest effect on the look of the shot. It can be placed on either side of the camera, fully lighting that side of the subject while casting shadows on the other side.

A **Fill light** is the secondary light source, typically softer and lower intensity than the key, and is placed on the opposite side of the key to fill in areas where hard shadows have been created.

A **Back light** is positioned behind the subject in order to provide illumination from the rear. This acts to better define the silhouette of the subject, separating it from the background and adding more depth and dimension to the scene. It can also be used to add highlights or a subtle glowing effect to the entire outline of the subject or perhaps an isolated area such as the crown of the head.

This is the fundamental 3-Point Lighting technique described in its most basic form. Depending on the size and nature of the shoot, you may only have one light to work with which will have to serve as your key light. If you have access to a light kit, you can then add the fill, back light, and whatever other applications best suit the needs of the project.

3-Point Lighting Technique

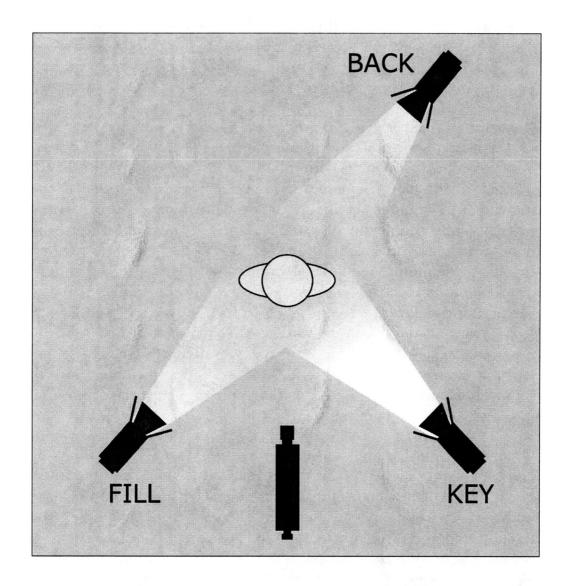

It can take quite a bit of time in order to get things just right when lighting a scene. This tends to drain the energy of performers when they are kept standing around the set for long periods of time while the scene is being lit. A **Stand-in** is a person who takes the place of an actor during shot set-ups while lighting adjustments are being performed on the set.

A **scrim** is a heatproof, translucent fabric, usually stretched across a frame of some sort, which is placed in front of a lighting instrument to diffuse the intensity of the light. In addition to placing a diffusion element, such as a scrim, in front of the instrument, another common method of softening a light's intensity is to adjust the spot/flood setting of the lamp toward the flood position. Thus resulting in a broader and less concentrated beam. A commonly available **dimmer switch** is also capable of quickly adjusting the intensity of a lighting instrument by regulating the flow of current going to it. However, it is important to be aware of the resulting change in color temperature and the potential impact it might have on the overall lighting of the scene. **Dulling spray** can sometimes be used to tone down the glare of highly reflective surfaces that either cause *hot spots* or in some other way distract from the shot.

On larger productions, additional lighting instruments may be used to light scenery, particular set elements, or the entire background of a scene. Lights are also used for other purposes such as creating special lighting effects — for example, the flashing red and blue lights of a police car or to simulate the pool of light emanating from a street lamp. Some of the most effectively executed lighting techniques are the ones that are so subtle and natural looking that they simply perform their intended function while going entirely unnoticed by the viewer.

CHAPTER SUMMARY

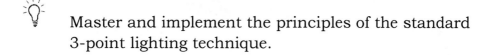 Master and implement the principles of the standard 3-point lighting technique.

Reflector boards can be used to effectively bounce available light onto a subject.

Take the time to get that little sparkle in the subject's eyes in order to add life and to avoid deadening their on-screen appearance unless going for a certain look.

Dimmer switches can adjust the intensity of a lighting instrument, but may also alter color temperature.

8

SOUND

PRODUCTION AUDIO

There is a phenomenon that exists in the production world that consistently holds true, almost without fail; the single most blatant and obvious indicator of a non-professional film or video production is *poor sound quality*. While you may be able to cover up the occasional shaky camera move, blend in some imperfect lighting conditions, or even "cut around" a less than spectacular acting performance, bad sound is unforgivable. This is because so much of the viewing experience is auditory in nature.

Many novice filmmakers make the mistake of focusing so much on the visual element of their craft [sometimes to the point of obsessing over the pursuit of complex camera moves or elaborate staging techniques for the sole purpose of getting visually impressive shots] that they pay little attention to the importance of capturing clean, quality source audio. Nothing screams *shoddy production* louder than poor sound quality. Furthermore, many editors would argue there are few things that are harder to fix in post-production.

A **Sound Mixer** is the technician responsible for the operation of the production's audio recording equipment. On smaller productions, you will most likely record sound directly to the camera either with the camera's *on-board* microphone or by using an external microphone that is connected to the camera. A **lavalier microphone** is a small microphone typically equipped with a clip so it can be easily fastened to a subject [and often concealed] for hands-free use. Commonly called a *Lav* or *Lapel Mic*, its cord can be hidden by clothing and is run to a transmitter pack/unit, which sends the signal by radio frequency to a receiver pack/unit that can be connected to the camera itself, a mixing console or some other audio recording device.

A **shotgun microphone** is a highly directional microphone that functions primarily to pick up sound directly in front of it. Shotgun mics are often used with a **boom** mount, sometimes called a fish pole, so that an operator can follow the sound by pointing the pick-up end of the mic in the direction of the audio source. When using a boom, it is important to keep the pick-up end of a unidirectional mic pointed directly at the mouth of the subject who is speaking.

An **omni-directional microphone** has a pick-up pattern that captures sound in all directions. Some uses for omni-directional mics include recording crowd noise, live theatre performances, and environmental sounds. In the photograph below, notice how the boom operator is positioning a unidirectional shotgun microphone so that it is pointing directly at the audio source.

Photo courtesy of ENDI ENTERTAINMENT, LLC.
Production still taken on the set of a promotional video shoot for the
CandidaMD.com website featuring John E. Humiston, M.D.

AMBIENT SOUND

Ambient sound refers to the background noises that are inherent to a particular location. When shooting at an outdoor location, the ambient sounds are referred to as *environmental* or *presence tracks*. At an inside location or on set it is called *room tone*. Ambiance can include sounds as subtle as the hum of a distant freeway or an air conditioning unit, or distinct noises like the nearby squawking of an exotic bird. It is important to record ambient sound at each location you shoot (30 to 60 seconds is usually sufficient). These tracks can then be *looped* in post and laid under their corresponding scenes for a realistic effect.

AUDIO CHECK

Always record some test audio before every shoot and play it back in the headphones to ensure that all of the microphones and other audio components are working properly. I have personally spent an entire day of shooting only to get back to the editing bay and discover there was no audio track recorded due to an overlooked camera setting. A simple test recording could have prevented this. Production sound should be continually monitored through high quality headphones that have been specifically designed and marketed for extreme isolation or noise cancelling applications to ensure that you are capturing a clean audio signal at all times. A **VU meter** (volume unit meter) provides a measurement of sound levels by approximating amplitude of an audio signal. If multiple VU meters occur at different points along the audio chain, such as on board the camera, field recorder, and even built into microphones, all will have to be monitored. It is important to watch for the needle spiking up beyond the normal range in order to avoid audio distortion. If an actor is going to be screaming in a scene or you know that some other excessively loud noise is going to occur, rehearse it for the sound mixer so that any necessary modifications can be made with regard to adjusting recording levels and/or microphone placement.

A **Field Recorder** is a device used to record audio separately from the picture. When this is done, the sound tracks will have to be synced with the picture in post-production before editing. Although digital audiotape recorders, or *DAT machines*, were once the standard in production audio, tapeless solid-state digital audio recording and data storage such as hard disc, or flash memory based formats are quickly replacing the older audiotape based technologies in many modern production applications.

A **clapboard** or **slate** is used to synchronize picture and sound, as well as identifying takes in a film production. To "slate" at the beginning of a take refers to the function of having a designated crewmember (usually an assistant camera person) snap shut the clapper "sticks" in front of the camera so that the sound and picture can be synced at a later time.

Timecode refers to a system of assigning a numeric identification to each frame of film. Standard timecode format consists of 4 sets of numbers, expressed as 01:24:38:01(hour:minute:second:frame), essentially acting as an address for that individual frame to make it easy to reference during editing. Fig 8.1 shows a traditional film slate with an erasable surface so that information can be easily changed between takes. Fig 8.2 shows a sync slate that is capable of syncing with the camera and has a built-in timecode display.

Traditional Film Slate

Digital Sync Slate

Fig 8.1

Fig 8.2

ADR

ADR (Automated Dialogue Replacement or **Additional Dialogue Recording)**, also known as **dubbing** or **looping**, is the process of re-recording passages of clean audio during post-production to replace the original audio captured during the shoot.

Typically, this becomes necessary in order to replace flawed source audio recorded on location. For example, the original audio may have been compromised by undesirable environmental sound conditions that were either unable to be controlled by the production or perhaps went unnoticed by the sound mixer.

Some other common purposes of ADR include:

o   Recording voice-over narration.

o   Dubbing over strong language in order to adapt a film for network broadcast.

o   Replacing all of the dialogue of a project in another language for foreign distribution.

o   Recording additional or missing lines of dialogue after principal photography has ended that were discovered to be necessary after the fact for any given number of reasons.

CHAPTER SUMMARY

▶ Do a test recording before the first shot of the day, and listen to the playback.

▶ Always use high quality, extreme isolation or noise cancelling headphones to monitor the sound at its final destination or at the device on which it is being recorded.

▶ Monitor all sound meters closely to avoid recording excessively loud sounds at levels that will result in audio distortion.

▶ Always use new batteries in all microphones and transmitter/receiver packs on every shoot.

▶ Record *environmental sounds* or *room tone* tracks at each separate shooting location.

▶ Be prepared to use ADR in post-production when necessary for applications such as doing voice-overs or operations involving the replacement of original dialogue tracks.

9

PRODUCTION

Production begins with the first day of principal photography, or *shooting*, and ends when the final image or sound has been captured. Now that a final shooting script has been secured, the talent has been cast, and a crew has been assembled, all of the hard work and preparation done in pre-production will start to pay off as filming begins. Elements that were covered in Chapter Three, such as the production schedule and shooting script, provide the roadmap you will follow throughout the production phase.

BEFORE THE SHOOT

Before we discuss the first day of production any further, it is worth emphasizing the importance of paying close attention to what gets done on the days leading up to shooting day one. *Preparation is key!* It is a good practice to schedule an equipment check the day before the shoot. At that time you can also go over a detailed checklist (like the one provided in the forms section at the back of this book) designed to include even the smallest and simplest detail of preparation before you load up and head off to location.

Also, you should be well-rested, hydrated and nourished before the shoot. Production days are long and tend to be much more physically and mentally demanding than most people might imagine. It is essential to have enough water and healthy snack food on hand for the entire cast and crew. Other must-haves include items such as sun block and umbrellas, if shooting outdoors, and a first-aid kit. No matter what the size and nature of the project, having secured one or more good production assistants will prove extremely valuable once filming begins.

BLOCKING

Blocking is a term that refers to the process of determining and rehearsing the physical positioning and movement of subjects as they will occur during a given scene or sequence. This is the time to map out all of the logistical concerns as far as who will stand or sit where, when an actor may cross from one point in the scene to another, or start or stop handling a prop, or performing a particular piece of business etc. A designated spot where an actor is to begin a scene or end up on after a planned movement is referred to as a *mark*. Gaffer's tape is often used to indicate such positions on the ground, as long as it will not be seen on camera.

REHEARSAL

One of the most important factors in getting the performance you want out of your talent is, in my opinion, scheduling dedicated rehearsal time. Unfortunately this crucial preparatory process is something that is not always given its proper due, and is therefore oftentimes done either very rapidly with little or no planning or, worse yet, overlooked altogether. Depending on the circumstances of the project, the need for a brief rehearsal vs. an extensive detail oriented one may vary. In any event, however, a realistic amount of time should be allocated in the shooting schedule for an adequate run-through of rehearsal takes.

Although actors are typically expected to come to the set with an understanding of the scene and in a well-prepared state, there are some things that just tend to get worked out during the rehearsal that are not always possible for an actor or performer to have already prepared on their own. Giving your talent the opportunity to run through the scene a few times and get comfortable with the environment has several important benefits. In addition to calming nerves, it is a great time during which new levels of creativity can be reached.

Perhaps one of the players will uncover new layers of their character during a rehearsal take that they were not previously aware of. Likewise, a director will often discover new meaning and layers within the scene that just seem to begin to taking shape while watching the cast rehearsing. Camera operators and other members of the technical crew will also benefit from the additional rehearsal takes in order to work out mechanical operations having to do with things such as shot composition, camera movement, and focus changes.

THE SHOOT

Whenever possible, you will want to arrive at the location early so you will have ample time to go over the shot list and address any logistical concerns you may have about the upcoming day's shooting schedule. If you and your team were diligent in your preparation, most potential concerns will have already been dealt with in advance. Nonetheless, it is a good idea to set aside briefing time to allow the Director, DP and AD the opportunity to discuss (and perhaps even walk through) the intended shot list for the day in order to ensure that everyone is on the same page. Last-minute adjustments to camera set-ups and possible miscommunications that can be addressed early on often prevent valuable time and resources from being wasted later in the day when things are moving at full speed and there will be no time to spare.

At first glance, a film production unit at work may appear to the inexperienced onlooker as quite a chaotic environment. Yet with all of the right pieces in place, a good film crew can function smoothly and efficiently like a well-oiled machine. Similar to the conductor of a symphony, a competent director sets the tone and pace of the entire company in order to turn out a finished product that reflects the collaborative effort of a group of artistic individuals.

WEARING MANY HATS

When working on smaller scale productions and with smaller crews, a director will end up performing a lot of tasks that would normally fall under the scope of other departments on a larger scale production. Directors who make the effort to learn as much as they can about each of the different aspects of the technical process of filmmaking early on, such as cinematography, lighting, editing, etc., tend to have an easier time communicating exactly what they expect from the heads of those departments when it comes time to work on a larger production with a full crew. After all, it is difficult to relate to and earn the respect of these individuals without first possessing a genuine understanding of the demands inherent to each of their jobs.

STAYING ON SCHEDULE

It is important to follow the production schedule and stick to your shot list in order to remain focused on getting all of the necessary takes you have planned for the day. You will have to trust your preparation and your AD's ability to keep you on track throughout the shooting day. In the event of bad weather on a day when exterior shots are planned, whenever possible there should already be provisions in place for a *Cover Set*.

Having a cover set essentially involves a backup plan for the company to move to another location, to get interior shots for example, until weather conditions improve or if necessary have the shooting schedule rearranged to accommodate the outdoor shots on another day. If this scenario is thought out in advance and some of the interior sets can be made tentatively available for multiple days, many times a simple switching of days in the shooting schedule can be done without throwing the whole production entirely off course.

WRAPPING IT UP

Before leaving any location, always perform a thorough canvassing of the area to be sure that nothing gets left behind. This process is commonly referred to as doing an "idiot check". Equally important is to see to it that any messes made by the production have been cleaned up and the area is restored to as good a condition as it was found, if not better. It is a good idea to treat the locations with the same respect you would if it were your own property. After all, you never know when you might need to return to re-shoot something, or simply want to be welcome to come back and use the location again on another project.

Once principal photography has been completed and all of the equipment has been packed up, the production phase will have essentially come to a close. Hence the phrase "That's a wrap!" Now it is time gather up all the pieces of the story puzzle, and start putting it all together.

CHAPTER SUMMARY

- Preparation is key! Perform a thorough equipment check and preparation session before shooting.

- Make provisions for a cover set in case of bad weather or the unexpected occurrence of other unforeseen conditions.

- Plan for a briefing at the top of the day with Director, DP and AD to go over the intended shot list in order to ensure that everyone is on the same page.

- Stick to the shooting schedule and trust your AD to keep you and the production on track.

- When it is time to wrap, check to be sure that nothing gets left behind and be sure to clean up after yourself and leave the location in as good condition as you found it.

10
POST-PRODUCTION

Post-production, often simply referred to as *post*, is the process that includes all remaining components of the filmmaking process that starts from the time the last shot has been captured on the final day of production and continues until the final output of the project is seen to completion.

EDITING

Editing is the process of selecting, arranging and assembling multiple camera takes or clips into a particular sequence or order of shots, as determined by the script. This also includes the incorporation of audio components and special effects. A **Non-linear editing system (NLE)** refers to a system of editing film or video that allows the editor to randomly access a frame or series of frames from the source material for assembly in any order so desired. The major difference between this and traditional film editing is that non-linear editing is a *non-destructive* process, whereas traditional editing requires the physical cutting of the negative, making it a *destructive* process. There are many computer based non-linear editing systems on the market. If you are considering a career as an editor, you may wish to do your own research to discover what systems are most prevalent in the particular area of the industry you wish to pursue. One of the greatest *advantages* of shooting digitally is the ability to shoot a great deal of footage at a relatively low cost. Likewise, one of the greatest *disadvantages* of shooting digitally is the ability to shoot a great deal of footage at a relatively low cost! Depending on your personal filmmaking style, you may be a fan of shooting tons of footage and then weeding out the gems through a process of elimination. Or, you may be more from the school of measuring twice and cutting once, opting to roll the camera for a smaller number of takes.

Perhaps you fall somewhere in between. Whatever your personal filmmaking style or philosophy may be, it is important to think about the editing process long before you set up a camera for the first shot of the day. You should be thinking about the finished product before creating a shot list, before doing your storyboards, and even before you lock your shooting script. Decisions you make during pre-production, as well as on the set, will have a great impact on what challenges you and your editor (which may end up being you) will have to deal with in post.

LOG AND CAPTURE

Logging and capturing is the process of bringing digital video footage into an editing system via an internal or external source (such as a deck, capture card, or media converter) or by connecting the camera directly to the system. If originating from a non-digital source, such as film, the footage must first be digitized before being transferred. Raw footage is typically captured in segments representing individual *takes*, or *clips*, and is then stored on hard drives. Properly numbering and slating scenes and takes during shooting is a crucial element in expediting this process efficiently. It is important to place the clips in bins that are systematically labeled and organized so they can be easily located at a later time.

When looking at raw footage, there are many variables an editor is sure to become faced with when it comes time to select one particular take or clip over another. It is my personal opinion that emotional truth, in the form of a believable performance, should reign supreme over most other considerations [save for extreme circumstances that might render a take useless, such as a crew member walking through the shot for example]. After all, if the very message of the piece fails to hit its mark or the viewer is not made to *feel* something, who really cares if you were able to use the only take during which a fish magically jumped out of the water in the background?

MUSIC AND SOUND EFFECTS

A **Sound Editor** is the person responsible for matching production sound with the picture in post, as well as mixing the audio tracks. In addition to the production audio, this is the time when tracks containing musical scores and supplemental sound effects can be added to the mix. Creative use of well-chosen and carefully placed music and sound effects will provide additional layers of realism, emotional impact, and overall production value to your project. Audio tracks consisting of specific sounds, such as breaking glass, gunshots, screeching car tires or the roar of a jet airplane can be purchased in pre-recorded and catalogued collections called **sound libraries**.

LICENSED MUSIC

If you wish to use a song or other recorded work in a production, then a *master use license* must be obtained from whomever owns the publishing rights to the recording. Depending on variables such as the specific intended use of the song, the popularity of the recording artist, and the scale of distribution of the project, the cost of acquiring such licensing can vary greatly. A search of song titles, artists, and publishers can be done through ASCAP.com or BMI.com in order to locate the owners of publishing rights to most modern recorded works, along with pertinent contact information.

ROYALTY-FREE MUSIC

Royalty-free music refers to recorded works that are purchased one time and may be used over and over again without limitation. There are many royalty-free soundtrack collections and sound effects libraries available that are reasonably priced and provide a wide variety of musical scores and sound effects.

MORE ON SOUNDTRACKING

A **Foley Artist** is a person who specializes in creating naturally occurring sounds to be recorded and added to a soundtrack in post-production. Foley artists work with a recording engineer in specially equipped recording studios in order to create and capture a wide variety of realistic sound effects. Recorded sound effects can be used to enhance the actual audio that was recorded on location, or to create an entire soundtrack from scratch. Some common examples of sounds captured on set that may require enhancement might be that of breaking glass, a door slamming shut, or crunching of footsteps walking through rustling leaves. Cartoons and animated features are good examples of productions that will typically contain a soundtrack entirely manufactured by the work of foley artists, sound designers and other post-production audio professionals.

DOING A TEST SCREENING

One of the best ways to gauge the effect your project will have on viewers is to do a *test screening*. Simply invite a group of friends, family, or other associates to a private screening of your project once you have assembled a rough cut that you feel comfortable showing. Offer to provide whatever beverages and snacks you can manage and let it roll. Watch and listen for the reaction of your audience, and welcome feedback and criticism after the viewing. It might even prove helpful to record video of the audience during and after the screening for future reference. Your audience may experience reactions to your project that you could not have otherwise predicted. This provides you invaluable information that may just end up having an impact on the finishing tweaks and adjustments to be made on the way to achieving the final cut. Most importantly, try not to take personal offense to any of the criticism and remember to take notes.

Keep in mind that this is a golden opportunity to test your project on a live audience and it is all for the purpose of making your picture the best that it can be. After all, you would much rather be made aware of your project's shortcomings as a result of the input of a small group of individuals, than have these flaws left in the final cut to be seen by your entire viewing audience after releasing the finished product.

EDITING WEB VIDEOS

As discussed earlier in the chapter on the script, we know that the attention spans of our Internet viewing audience tend to be on the shorter side. Just as the writing preparation of web-based content often requires us to get to the point and keep up the pace, the Internet content savvy editor will often cater to this end by incorporating elements such as faster cuts and bold visuals in order to deliver a simple, clear, and direct message in a relatively short amount of time. Even if at times it will only be viewed on a small screen, like that of a mobile phone.

You will also want to take the matter of screen size into account when it comes time to add titles. Item such as text, logo, or other graphic elements should appear large enough to be easily seen on the smallest of screens. Finally, you will want to test screen your final product on several devices and across multiple viewing platforms in order to see just how it plays. Be sure to pay special attention to sound quality and levels.

CHAPTER SUMMARY

✎   Be thinking about the editing process long before the shoot begins.

✎   Keep picture and sound clips neatly organized in bins during logging and capturing.

✎   Emotional truth and believable performances are top priorities when selecting takes for use in the final edit.

✎   Well-placed music and sound effects add realism, emotional impact and production value to a project.

✎   Royalty-free music and soundtrack collections are great ways to access a variety of professional grade music and sound effects.

✎   Consider doing a test screening of a rough cut to gauge how your project will affect viewers, and gather feedback afterward.

EPILOGUE

MOVING ON

As you go forward, it is important not to lose sight of the very purpose of producing film and video projects — the *Story*. It does not matter in what capacity I find myself involved with a creative project, serving the story first always remains my primary objective. This requires full participation in what must certainly be a collaborative *and* cooperative artistic effort. Dedication and sacrifice will be needed on behalf of all of the members of the team, which often (if not always) involves putting personal agendas and egos aside. I can honestly say there are few things I have experienced that can compare to the feeling of exhilaration that comes from being part of a group of individuals all working selflessly toward a common goal of creative excellence.

GETTING OTHERS ON BOARD

When it comes time to go into production it is always helpful to have extra hands on deck (as long as they are helpful hands, of course). Practice your "pitching" technique by telling people about the project in a way that gets them as excited about working on it as you are. A lot of people will jump at the chance to be a part of something creative and will often times participate in exchange for a screen credit. Especially if they themselves are interested in pursuing a filmmaking career or some other media arts related endeavor. Meals can be a good incentive too, as well as a copy of the finished work (only if and when, of course, it is appropriate for you to distribute them). Keep a current contact list and maintain social networking ties with other filmmakers, actors, and aspiring artists and make a note of each individual's strengths and particular areas of expertise. Such a talent pool will go a long way in helping you assemble the best possible cast and crew for every film or video project you produce.

LEARN HOW TO EDIT

Another invaluable skill to possess as a producer or director is editing. At the very least you will want to develop a basic proficiency in one of the many popular non-linear editing programs. I learned to edit during post-production on *Call Me Crazy*, the first independent short film that I worked on as a producer. This training did not occur because I had an instantaneous burst of inspiration to want to learn editing. It was born out of economic necessity because, quite honestly, we simply ran out of money on the project and could not afford to pay an editor. Never underestimate the cost of post-production!

As with most undertakings in life, the more you can learn to do for yourself, the less dependent you will become on others. Even if you plan to outsource the editing duties on all of your projects, having a good working knowledge of the process will often times allow you to better communicate your specific vision to the person doing the editing. Thus maintaining a greater level of creative control and ultimately resulting in the final output of the very picture and product that you have been visualizing since the inception of the project.

WRITE YOUR OWN MATERIAL

Keep in mind that good material to work with is not always going to be easy to come by. Great material is even more rare, and in the real world of motion picture making, not only does it tend to be in short supply, it can also get quite expensive. One of the best ways to maintain creative control of your projects is to be actively involved with the writing process. Now more than ever, today's filmmakers must wear as many hats as possible. Even if you do not consider yourself a writer by trade, it is important to be involved in this process by continuing to hone your skills in the areas of script analysis and story development — and write often.

THE TWO BOTTOM LINES

There are two ways by which the success of a film or video project will ultimately be judged. Therefore, there are essentially two bottom lines to be considered when working in the world of production. One bottom line has to do with telling the story in a way that makes the viewer *feel* something while effectively communicating the intended message. Yet another bottom line has to do with careful management of the almighty dollar throughout the process.

I still maintain and will continue to encourage that producers always be looking for new ways to get the most bang for their buck while wearing the producer's hat. After all, that is what *good* producers do. With that said, one must also remain true to the story, message, and meaning that is the very life-blood of the project being produced. Learning to balance between the elements of quality, speed, and cost-effectiveness is a talent that not only can be difficult to master, but at times will seem all but impossible. That is what a *great* producer does. It is in the very presence of the pursuit of such balance that often results in an environment that is ripe for creative excellence. In my experience, that has always been when the real magic happens.

SHORT FILM PROJECT

In this project you will produce a two to three minute narrative short film from script to screen, utilizing the principles and techniques in this book. As an alternative, or perhaps in addition to this assignment, you may opt to shoot a public service announcement or a music video. You might already have access to music you can use that is licensed through your school, or maybe you have a contact with local musicians who are willing to cooperate in order to help promote one of their songs. Whatever the project you choose, the first step will be to acquire and develop the script. Begin by answering the following questions:

    o   What story will your film be telling and what is the central theme?

    o   What demographic makes up your target audience? (Males18-35, Young Families, Retirees etc).

    o   Where will the final product be viewed?

If you haven't already done so, now is the time to put together your crew and divide up responsibilities accordingly. When working with a small crew or in groups within a class setting, expect everyone to perform the functions of multiple job titles. Most importantly — work as a team!

Short Film Project Checklist

☐   Script Development   Deadline: _____

☐   Casting Notices   Posted on: _____

☐   Casting Session   Held on: _____

☐   Shooting Schedule   Due by: _____

☐   Storyboard   Due by: _____

☐   Shot List   Due by: _____

☐   Filming   Date(s): _____

☐   Editing & Music   Due by: _____

GLOSSARY OF TERMS

Above the Line Costs – costs in the budget of a film project associated with creative personnel such as producer(s), director, writer(s) and lead actors.

Actor – any (male, female or animal) performer that appears in a production (a.k.a. **talent**).

ADR / Automatic Dialogue Replacement or Additional Dialogue Recording (see also **Dubbing**, **Looping**) – the process of re-recording passages of clean audio during post-production to replace the original audio captured during the shoot.

Ambient Sound – background noises and environmental sounds inherent to a particular location.

Animal Handler – person in charge of any animals on the set (a.k.a. **Animal Wrangler**).

Art Director – individual who works closely with and under the direction of the production designer to help carry out their vision.

Aspect Ratio – refers to the dimensions of an image on screen, determined by how it was shot and arrived at by dividing its width by its height, expressed Width:Height.

Back Light – secondary light source positioned behind the subject in order to better define the silhouette of the subject, separating it from the background and adding more depth and dimension to the scene.

Below the Line Costs – costs in the budget of a film project other than the *above the line costs* (e.g. remaining cast, crew, props, equipment rental, craft services).

Best Boy Grip – the key grip's main assistant or "right-hand" person.

Blocking – term that refers to the process of determining and rehearsing the physical positioning and movement of subjects as they will occur during a given scene or sequence.

Boom – a portable extension device or pole, often adjustable in length, typically used by an operator to follow an audio source with a directional microphone mounted to it, but may also be outfitted with a light fixture or camera (a.k.a. **Boom Pole**).

Boom Operator – technician in charge of handling the boom mic.

Bounce Light – light from a primary source that is reflected off of some other surface and re-directed onto a subject or scene.

Callback – subsequent audition(s) an actor has been invited to at the request of the director or producer(s).

Casting – the process of selecting and hiring actors to appear in a production.

Clapboard – device used to synchronize picture and sound, as well as identifying takes in a film production (*See* **Slate**).

Close-Up (CU) – shot convention usually framing a subject from the shoulders up.

Copy – refers to pages of television or radio commercial scripts.

Coverage – shots and camera angles that are needed in addition to the master shot, including reverse angles, close-ups and inserts.

Depth of Field – refers to the area (i.e. vertical plane of space) in front of the camera in which the objects seen by the camera are in focus.

Director of Photography (DP) – person responsible for the mechanical aspects of camera placement, movement, operation and lighting exposure.

Dimmer Switch – electrical device used to regulate the flow of current in order to control the intensity of a lighting instrument.

Director – person responsible for overseeing all of the creative aspects of a film production.

Dolly/Trucking Shot – a moving shot taken from a camera that is mounted on a wheeled platform that is usually hydraulically powered (often referred to as a *dolly* or *truck*) that typically rides on rails (a.k.a. tracks) so that the camera can move smoothly and quietly during operation (a.k.a. **Follow Shot** or **Tracking Shot**).

Dubbing (*See* **ADR**)

Editing – the process of selecting, arranging and assembling multiple camera takes or clips (including audio components) into a particular sequence or order of shots, as determined by the script.

Establishing Shot – shot composition that captures the primary action or setting of a scene in its entirety (a.k.a. **Long Shot**).

Extreme Close-Up (ECU) – shot convention even closer in proximity than a Close Up, often used to isolate the image of a particular object or feature (e.g. the eyes or mouth of a subject).

Field Recorder – device used for recording production audio separately from the picture to be synced up later for editing.

Fill Light – secondary light source placed on the opposite side from the key light to fill in shadows created by the key.

Film Permit – certificate issued by a local film office, commission or other authorized agency granting permission to film within a given jurisdiction.

Focus – refers to the sharpness, clarity and distinctness of an image.

Foley Artist – specializes in creating naturally occurring sounds to be recorded and added to a soundtrack in post-production.

Gaffer – person responsible for the placement and operation of lighting instruments and fixtures, under the direction of the DP.

Green Screen (or **Blue Screen**) – a monochromatic background that can easily be replaced with other images in post-production.

Grip – member of the crew responsible for multiple jobs such as setting up camera cranes, laying dolly tracks, moving props or scenery pieces as well as moving and maintaining any other equipment that may be in use on the set.

Insert – a shot within a sequence or scene that is usually close-up in orientation and intended to draw the viewer's attention to a piece of visual information of particular importance to the story.

Jib Arm – a counterweighted camera mounting system, typically supported by a dolly, tripod or other mounting platform, used to increase the camera's range of motion.

Key Grip – head grip in charge of coordinating the efforts of all other grips on the crew, working under the direction of the gaffer. The key grip's main assistant is known as the *Best Boy Grip*.

Key Light – primary light source used to illuminate the scene, having the greatest effect on the look of the shot.

Location – an existing place to which a film company or crew travels in order to shoot some or all of a production [on location].

Location Release – signed agreement giving expressed written permission to use the image and likeness of the location in the making of a film project.

Log and Capture – function of bringing digital video footage into an editing system either by connecting the camera directly to the system or through a tape deck.

Looping (*See* **ADR**)

Makeup Artist – individual trained in the application and use of makeup specifically for TV and film production.

Master Shot – a continuous shot (or *take*) that captures the primary action or setting of a scene.

Medium Close-Up (MCU) – shot composition framing a subject from the chest area up (a.k.a. ***Bust Shot***).

Medium Shot – shot composition usually framing a subject from just below the waist up.

Non-Linear Editing System (NLE) – a system of editing film or video that allows the editor to randomly access any frame or series of frames from the source material for re-assembly.

Off-Screen (O.S.) – refers to recorded dialogue of a character that is in the scene, but out of camera range.

Pan – a camera move from side to side [left to right or right to left].

Personal Release – a signed agreement giving expressed written permission to use a person's image and likeness (including their recorded voice) in the making and promotion of a film project.

Post-production – the process that includes all components of the filmmaking process that take place from the time the last shot has been captured on the final day of production until the final output of the project (a.k.a. *Post*).

Pre-production – all components of the filmmaking process that take place from the very inception of a given project up until the first day of principal photography.

Producer – individual in charge of overseeing a film production.

Production – phase during which the principal photography takes place to capture the images that will be used in a film project.

Production Assistant – Individual that performs a multitude of various functions and tasks during the course of a production.

Production Insurance – insurance policy that provides liability and other forms of coverage for a film production.

Production Value – the collective result of elements that provide a final product that is of high quality and has the appearance of taking a lot of time and/or money to produce.

Reflector Board – reflective surface area used to re-direct light onto a subject.

Room Tone – environmental sound track recorded at an inside location.

Scrim – a translucent, heatproof fabric that is placed in front of a lighting instrument to diffuse the light.

Script – the written text of a filmed production that details out the story along with its setting, sequence of events as well as the actions and dialogue of the actors.

Set – the physical environment in which the filmed action takes place. Sets may be interior or exterior locales, and are usually artificially manufactured places that are constructed for the production.

Set Decorator – person in charge of designing, overseeing and setting up the artistic elements of a film set.

Set Designer – individual who designs and prepares blueprints and mechanical drawings in order to illustrate in detail the technical elements associated with a set's construction.

Shooting Script – a final version of a script with scenes numbered and arranged in the order they are to be shot according to the shooting schedule.

Shot List – a list of all the shots needed from every camera angle, for every scene of a day's shooting schedule.

Sides – select scenes or pages taken from a script, usually for purposes of auditioning actors.

Slate (*See* **Clapper Board**)

Sound Editor – person responsible for matching production sound with the picture in post, as well as mixing the audio tracks.

Sound Library – collection of pre-recorded sound effects.

Sound Mixer – technician responsible for the operation of the production's audio recording equipment (a.k.a. **Sound Recordist**).

Soundstage – a spacious, enclosed space or building in a studio facility dedicated for use in film productions that provides a great deal of control over environmental factors such as sound, lighting, climate and set security.

Stabilization System (Camera) – specially designed mounting rigs, usually attached to a harness worn by the operator, to facilitate smooth camera movements.

Still Photographer – person(s) charged with capturing still images in order to document elements of the production taking place both on set and behind the scenes.

Storyboard – a visual representation, typically in the form of several illustrations, each of which captures the essence of the primary images that will tell the story, usually in chronological order.

Stand-in – individual who takes the place of an actor on the set during shot set-ups and while lighting adjustments are performed.

Talent – term commonly used to refer to actors in a production.

Tilt – a camera move in either an upward or downward motion.

Timecode – refers to a system of assigning a numeric identification to each frame of film.

Voice Over (V.O.) – refers to recorded dialogue or narration of a character or narrator that is not seen by the viewer.

VU Meter – (Volume Unit Meter) provides a measurement of sound levels by approximating amplitude of an audio signal.

White Balance – color balancing function that gives the camera a reference to *true white*, so that objects that are white will be captured and recorded accurately.

Zoom-In/Zoom-Out – the changing of perspective by "pushing in" or "pulling back" achieved mechanically inside the camera, either digitally or with the aid of a lens with a variable focal length lens.

RESOURCES & SUGGESTED READING

General Film and Video Production/Directing:

10 Step Video Production: Make a Music Video, Commercial, or Short Film in 10 Simple Steps
De Veau Dunn (10 Step Media)

On Film-making: An Introduction to the Craft of the Director
Alexander Mackendrick (Faber & Faber)

Power Filmmaking Kit
Jason Tomaric (Focal Press)

The Shut Up and Shoot Documentary Guide: A Down & Dirty DV Production
Anthony Q. Artis (Focal Press)

Producing/Production Management:

Film Production Management 101 – 2nd Edition: Management & Coordination in a Digital Age
Deborah Patz (Michael Wiese Productions)

The Independent Film Producer's Survival Guide: A Business and Legal Sourcebook
Gunnar Erickson (Schirmer G Books)

Cinematography/Shot Composition:

Five C's of Cinematography: Motion Picture Filming Techniques
Joseph V. Mascelli (Silman-James Press)

Master Shots: 100 Advanced Camera Techniques to Get an Expensive Look on Your Low-Budget Movie
Christopher Kenworthy (Michael Wiese Productions)

Sound Engineering/Production Audio:

Producing Great Sound for Film and Video, 3rd Edition (DV Expert Series)
Jay Rose (Focal Press)

Sound for Digital Video
Tomlinson Holman (Focal Press)

Lighting for Film and Video Production:

Motion Picture and Video Lighting 2nd Edition
Blaine Brown (Focal Press)

Painting With Light
John Alton (University of California Press)

Screenwriting/Story and Character Development:

Screenplay
Syd Field (Dell Publishing)

Story: Structure, Substance, Style and The Principals of Screenwriting
Robert McKee (Regan Books/HarperCollins Publishing)

Acting/Working with Actors:

Directing Actors: Creating Memorable Performances for Film & Television
Judith Weston (Michael Wiese Productions)

I'll Be In My Trailer: The Creative Wars Between Directors and Actors
John Badham & Craig Modderno (Michael Wiese Productions)

Michael Caine - Acting in Film: An Actor's Take on Movie Making
Michael Caine (Applause Books)

Sample
PRODUCTION FORMS

PRODUCTION BREAKDOWN SHEET

SHOT LIST

CONTINUITY LOG

EDITOR'S LOG

PERSONAL RELEASE FORM

LOCATION RELEASE FORM

MINOR RELEASE FORM

EQUIPMENT CHECKLIST

AUDITION SIGN-IN SHEET

PERFORMER SIZE CARD

CALL SHEET

STORYBOARD TEMPLATE

NOTICE—DISCLAIMER: Provided in this section are *sample* production forms that you are free to use as *guidelines* in order to create customized forms to suit the needs of your production. The author/publisher of this book DOES NOT provide legal advice or services of any kind. Always consult an attorney or other qualified professional in order to ensure that the release agreements you intend to use are properly prepared and are acceptable for use at the time and locale of your production.

PRODUCTION BREAKDOWN SHEET

TITLE: _____   DAY   NIGHT   SHEET:

| DAYS _____ |
| PAGES _____ |
| STAGE _____ |
| LOCATION _____ |

SYNOPSIS

NOTES

MUSIC / SOUND EFFECTS

SPECIAL EFFECTS

VEHICLES

ANIMALS

CAST

EXTRAS

PROPS

SHOT LIST

PRODUCTION TITLE:			DATE:
DIRECTOR:			PAGE: of

SHOT#	SCENE#	INT./EXT.	ONE-LINE DESCRIPTION

NOTES:

SCRIPT SUPERVISOR'S CONTINUITY LOG

PRODUCTION TITLE:	DATE:
DIRECTOR:	SHOOT DAY: of

SCENE	TAKE	TIME	LENS	AUDIO	PRINT	ACTION

SCRIPT SUPERVISOR:	SIGNED:

EDITIOR'S LOG

PRODUCTION/TITLE:	DATE:
DIRECTOR:	DAY:
SCRIPT SUPERVISOR:	DAY: of

ROLL	SCENE	TAKE	D / N	TIME IN	TIME OUT	REMARKS

PERSONAL RELEASE

FOR VALUABLE CONSIDERATION, including the agreement to produce the programs(s)

tentatively titled _____

I hereby irrevocably grant to _____, "the Producer", its

licenses, agents, successors and assigns, the right (but not the obligation), in perpetuity throughout

the world, in all media, now or hereafter known, to use (in any manner it deems appropriate, and

without limitation) in and in connection with the program, by whatever means exhibited, advertised

or exploited: my appearance in the program, still photographs of me, recordings of my voice taken or

made of me by it, any music sung or played by me, and my actual or fictitious name.

On my own behalf, and on behalf of my heirs, next of kin, executors, administrators, successors, and

assigns, I hereby release the Filmmaker, its agents licenses, successors and assigns, from any and all

claims, liabilities and damages arising out of the rights granted hereunder, or the exercise thereof.

_____
Date

Witness Signed
_____

Witness Printed
_____

Signature
_____

Printed Name
_____

Street Address
_____

City, State, Zip Code
_____

Phone Number

LOCATION RELEASE

FOR VALUABLE CONSIDERATION, including the agreement to produce the programs(s) currently

titled _____

I hereby irrevocably grant to _____ "the Producer", its licenses, agents, successors and assigns, the right (but not the obligation), in perpetuity throughout the world, in all media, now or hereafter known, to use (in any manner it deems appropriate, and without limitation) in and in connection with the program, by whatever means exhibited, advertised or exploited: the right to photograph, reproduce and use the exteriors and interiors of the premises located at:

_____ and to bring personnel and equipment on to the premises and to remove the same.

This is in connection with the production tentatively titled _____ and includes the right to re-use the images in connection with other motion pictures as the Producer, its successors, assigns and licensees shall elect, and, in connection with the exhibition, advertising and promotion thereof, in any manner whatsoever and at any time in any part of the world.

The Producer agrees to hold me/us free from any claims for damage or injury arising during its occupancy of the premises and arising out of its negligence thereon, and to leave the premises in as good order and condition as received by me/us, reasonable wear and tear, and use herein permitted excepted.

I/we acknowledge that, in photographing the premises, the Producer is not in any way depicting or portraying me/us in the production, either directly or indirectly. I/we will not assert or maintain against the Producer any claim of any kind or nature whatsoever, including, without limitation, those based upon invasion of privacy or other civil rights, defamation, libel or slander, in connection with the exercise of the permission herein granted.

I/we represent that I/we are the owner(s) and/or authorized representative(s) of the premises, and that I/we have the authority to grant the Producer the permission and rights herein, and that no other permission is required.

_____   _____
Signature (Owner or Authorized Agent)   Date

_____   _____
Printed Name (Owner or Authorized Agent)   Phone/Contact

_____
Location Address / Business Name (if applicable)

_____
Witness Signature

_____
Witness Printed Name

MINOR RELEASE

Name of Minor: _____ Guardian: _____
(Name Printed)

Address: _____

Phone/Contact: _____ SSN/Fed ID#: _____

Position/Title: _____ Weekly Rate: _____

Start Date: _____ Est. Finish Date: _____

Additional Terms: _____

Screen Credit: (End Credits): _____

I/We, the undersigned, am/are the parent(s) or guardian(s) of _____,

a minor child. I/We, the undersigned, being of legal age, do herby consent and grant to the Filmmaker

permission to use the likeness of _____, my/our _____

in connection with the production under the current working title of _____

and the perpetual right to use or to put the finished pictures, negatives, reproductions and copies or the

original prints and negatives of him/her and any recordings of his/her voice, including the right to

substitute the voice of other persons for his/her voice, his/her name or likeness in connection with the

exhibition, advertising, exploitation or any other use of such production or recording of his/her voice,

to any legitimate use the Filmmaker may deem proper.

I/We further agree and warrant that _____, the above-mentioned minor,
(Child's Name)
will not disaffirm or disavow said consent and permission on the ground that he/she was a minor on the

date of execution thereof or any similar grounds whatsoever, or endeavor to recover from you personally

or through any guardian, any sums for participating in the above entitled production.

Signature of Guardian: _____ Date: _____

Signature of Witness: _____ Date: _____

EQUIPMENT CHECKLIST

☐ **CAMERA EQUIPMENT:**

    ☐ CAMERA(S) ☐ POWER CORD(S)/ADAPTOR(S)

☐ **CAMERA ACCESSORIES:**

    ☐ MOUNTS ☐ TRIPOD ☐ CRANE/JIB ☐ DOLLY/TRACK
    ☐ LENS KIT ☐ FILTERS ☐ MATTE BOX ☐ CABLES

☐ **SOUND EQUIPMENT:**

    ☐ SHOTGUN MIC ☐ LAVS ☐ OTHER MICS ☐ WINDSCREEN
    ☐ HEADPHONES ☐ CABLES ☐ ADAPTORS ☐ BATTERIES

☐ **LIGHTING EQUIPMENT:**

    ☐ LIGHTING INSTRUMENTS ☐ EXTRA GLOBES ☐ DIMMERS
    ☐ STANDS ☐ CLAMPS ☐ SANDBAGS ☐ GLOVES
    ☐ GEL KIT ☐ SCRIMS ☐ FLAGS ☐ VISQUEEN
    ☐ GENERATOR ☐ FUEL ☐ EXTENSION CORDS

☐ **GRIP SUPPLIES:**

    ☐ TOOL KIT ☐ TAPE ☐ APPLE BOXES ☐ ROPE ☐ C-47's

☐ **SCENERY:**

    ☐ PROPS ☐ SET DRESSING ☐ ART SUPPLIES

☐ **MISC./OTHER:**

    ☐ _____
    ☐ _____
    ☐ _____

AUDITION SIGN-IN

PRODUCTION/TITLE:	DATE:

NAME	PHONE	AGENCY	UNION(S)	TIME IN

PERFORMER SIZE CARD

LEGAL NAME _____ **DATE** _____

PHONE _____ **EMAIL** _____

LOCAL ADDRESS _____

WOMEN:

_____	_____	_____	_____
Age	**Height**	**Weight**	**Dress**

_____	_____	_____	_____
Bust	**Waist**	**Hips**	**Shoe**

MEN:

_____	_____	_____	_____
Age	**Height**	**Weight**	**Suit**

_____	_____	_____	_____
Shirt (neck)	**Shirt (sleeve)**	**Waist**	**Inseam**

PHOTO

CALL SHEET

PRODUCTION TITLE:

DATE:	DAY:	DAY: of	CALL TIME:

DIRECTOR:	PHONE:
PRODUCER(S):	PHONE:
UPM:	PHONE:
1ST AD	PHONE:
LOC. MNGR:	PHONE:
LOCATION ADDRESS:	

SET/LOC. DESCRIPTION	SCENE	CAST	PAGE(S)	D/N

	CAST	ROLE OF	MAKEUP CALL	SET CALL	SCENES
1					
2					
3					
4					
5					
6					
7					
8					
9					

ATMOSPHERE / STAND-INS	SET CALL	COMMENTS

PREPARED/APPROVED BY (INITIALS)

1st AD:	UPM:	PRODUCER:

STORYBOARD

Project:

SCENE/SHOT: _____

SCENE/SHOT: _____

SCENE/SHOT: _____

SCENE/SHOT: _____

SCENE/SHOT: _____

SCENE/SHOT: _____

SCENE/SHOT: _____

SCENE/SHOT: _____

ABOUT THE AUTHOR

Nicholas George began his entertainment career at an early age as a working actor in addition to writing sketch comedy and collaborating with other writers on several screenplays. While studying performance arts in Southern California, he developed a passion for the behind-the-scenes elements of film production, and shifted his focus to producing short films, commercials and other independent film and video projects. He went on to complete a performing arts degree as well as more concentrated coursework in film and video production. Nicholas continues to wear the hats of writer, producer, and script consultant on several projects in various stages of development. He has a reputation for not compromising the integrity of the creative process, maintaining a high standard of production value, and above all else — always insisting on *serving the story first*!

NOTES

CPSIA information can be obtained at www.ICGtesting.com
Printed in the USA
BVOW06s0855131113

336200BV00004B/113/P